knit & purl

THE HARMONY GUIDES

knit & purl

250 stitches to knit

edited by Erika Knight

INTERWEAVE PRESS.
interweavebooks.com

First published in the United States by
Interweave Press LLC
201 East Fourth Street
Loveland, CO 80537-5655
Interweavebooks.com

Library of Congress Cataloging-in-Publication Data

Harmony guides. Knit and purl : 250 stitches to knit / Erika Knight,
editor.
      p. cm.
  Includes bibliographical references and index.
  ISBN 978-1-59668-056-2 (pbk. : alk. paper)
  1. Knitting--Patterns. I. Knight, Erika.
  TT825.H39725 2007
  746.43'2041--dc22
                                                    2007023165

10 9 8 7 6 5 4 3 2

Reproduction by Dot Gradations Ltd
Printed and bound by SNP Leefung Printers Ltd, China

contents

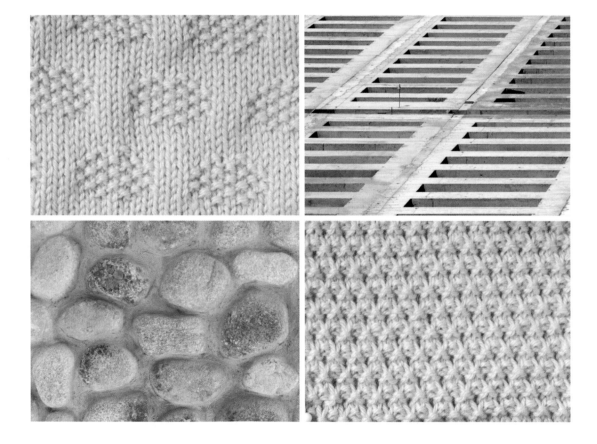

inspiration

Knit and purl, stitched in combination, can be configured into patterns and constructed into all kinds of fabrics. Texture is the inspiration for this edition.

For more than thirty years, *The Harmony Guides* have been a fountain of knitting knowledge and an authority on stitches. I've found them indispensable over the years, often turning to them to solve technical problems and to generate new ideas.

When I was asked to be involved with the makeover of the Harmony Guides just last year, I jumped at the chance to work with one of knitting's leading brands. After all, it was an opportunity to contribute as a designer, to add a few new stitches, and to edit the book through and through. The editors, designers, and I were thrilled to inject some new life to a beloved treasure. Harmony Guides would be in the spotlight once again.

The new Harmony Guides is a stitch-driven series. Each volume brims with 250 stitches to continually inspire and constantly challenge the knitter. I like to keep things simple, so this new collection is your quintessential guide to browse through or dip in and out of, and always there for you when you need it! I also couldn't resist scooping up old favorites—tried, tested, and trusted stitches—as well as adding

a few new ones to keep you inspired. Afterall, inspiration is the key to great design.

As a designer, I've always been drawn to textures in landscapes, from the city to the country to the coast. The simplest object or seemingly mundane item can provoke a new swatch idea or an entire collection. Whether you're a knitting novice who is picking up a pair of needles for the first time, or a seasoned professional with years of experience, if you are passionate about knitting, you will find inspiration and technical know how within these pages—there is always something to learn and to pass on.

If you're creating a pullover for a man, for example, there are certain traditional stitches associated with knits for men: ribs, cables, and arans especially, derived from the Guernsey and Aran Islands. However, garter stitch bars, fancy diamond patterns, mock ribs, and mock cables offer the same effect without the heavy and bulky weight. When designing, consider traditional stitches with a contemporary twist. Whether it be with colored cuffs, a textured collar, or color-blocked sleeves, traditional knitting can be constantly updated. Experiment with a new stitch pattern to create a new favorite sweater—it's a great excuse for buying more yarn and picking up your needles.

Knitting for women can be quite different, as anything goes! Women are as diverse in their tastes and moods as the stitches, colors, and yarns used for the design. Sometimes we like to wear classic; for other occasions, we may prefer something glamorous. When creating a piece for a daughter, a mother, or a friend, take the time to consider how the design might complement her personality. Timeless designs favor simple and discrete stitches with the focus on great detailing, and a good classic can be knitted time and time again just by changing the yarn or color. Experimental stitches, yarns, and colors can create a more individual or expressive piece and can be used to update a seasonal wardrobe.

For babies and toddlers, select stitches with care and avoid stitches with too many holes, which may tangle little fingers and toes. Basic stitches such as seed stitch, basket stitch, and simple small-scale textures are ideal, while garter stitch is very easy for the novice knitter or new mom. Think about comfort too and chose natural fibers. With simple stitches and simpler shapes, you may actually finish the piece before baby is born!

If you're keen to design for the home, knitted throws and cushions are modern classics and make great projects to experiment with stitches. Choose from smooth stockinette stitch, textured moss stitch, or even a rib or check stitch—a group of cushions knitted in the same yarn and color but different stitches would look luxurious on a bed or living room sofa. Tied with a big bow, they would make a fabulous personalised wedding gift for a friend.

From a technical standpoint, each of these stitches has been tried and tested to ensure accuracy. We've included some old favorites and provided a few new ones as well. If you're new to knitting, a section devoted to basic skills will ease the process. The key is to continue at it, and through trial and error you will discover the endless design possibilities at your fingertips. Knitting is not just a hobby, it can also be a lifestyle.

We all crave a little individuality in our often de-personalised environments and to create something with a pair of needles and a ball of yarn is very liberating. Enjoy the book and discover the endless combinations of patterns which can be created with two little stitches: knit and purl.

tools & equipment

To master any skill, it's imperative to have a solid foundation of the techniques. This section provides useful information that can come in handy while knitting.

Knitting Needles

Knitting needles are used in pairs to produce a flat knitted fabric. They are pointed at one end to form the stitches and have a knob at the other to retain the stitches. They may be made in plastic, wood, steel, or alloy and range in size from 2mm to 17mm in diameter. In England, needles used to be sized by numbers—the higher the number, the smaller the needle. In America, the opposite is true—higher numbers indicate larger sizes. Metric sizing has now been internationally adopted. Needles are also made in different lengths that will comfortably hold the stitches required for each project. It is useful to have a range of sizes so that gauge swatches can be knitted up and compared. Discard any needles that become bent. Points should be fairly sharp; blunt needles reduce the speed and ease of working.

Circular and double-pointed needles are used to produce a tubular fabric or flat rounds. Many traditional fisherman's sweaters are knitted in the round. Double-pointed needles are sold in sets of four or five. Circular needles consist of two needles joined by a flexible length of plastic. The plastic varies in length. Use the shorter lengths for knitting sleeves, neckbands, etc, and the longer lengths for larger pieces such as sweaters and skirts.

Cable needles are short needles used to hold the stitches of a cable to the back or front of the main body of knitting.

Needle gauges are punched with holes corresponding to the needle sizes and are marked with both the old numerical sizing and the metric sizing so you can easily check the size of any needle.

Stitch holders resemble large safety pins and are used to hold stitches while they are not being worked—for example, around a neckline when the neckband stitches will be picked up and worked after back and front have been joined. As an alternative, thread a blunt-pointed sewing needle with a generous length of contrast-colored yarn, thread it through the stitches to be held while they are still on the needle, then slip the stitches off the needle and knot both ends of the contrast yarn to secure the stitches.

Wool sewing needles or tapestry needles are used to sew completed pieces of knitting together. They are large with a broad eye for easy threading and a blunt point that will slip between the knitted stitches without splitting and fraying the yarn. Do not use the sharp-pointed sewing needles to sew up knitting.

A row counter is used to count the number of rows that have been knitted. It is a cylinder with a numbered dial that is pushed onto the needle and the dial is turned at the completion of each row.

A tape measure is essential for checking the gauge swatches and for measuring the length and width of completed knitting. For an accurate result, always smooth the knitting (without stretching) on a firm flat surface before measuring it.

A crochet hook is useful for picking up dropped stitches.

Knitting Yarn

Yarn is the term used for strands of spun fiber that are twisted together into a continuous length of the required thickness. Yarn can be of animal origin (wool, angora, mohair, silk, alpaca), vegetable origin (cotton, linen), or man-made (nylon, acrylic, rayon). Knitting yarn may be made up from a combination of different fibers.

Each single strand of yarn is known as a ply. A number of plys are twisted together to form the yarn. The texture and characteristics of the yarn may be varied by the combination of fibers and by the way in which the yarn is spun. Wool and other natural fibers are often combined with man-made fibers to make a yarn that is more economical and hard-wearing. Wool can also be treated to make it machine washable. The twist of the yarn is firm and smooth and knits up into a hard-wearing fabric. Loosely twisted yarn has a softer finish when knitted.

Buying Yarn

Yarn is most commonly sold wound into balls of specific weight measured into grams or ounces. Some yarn, particularly very thick yarn, is also sold in a coiled hank or skein that must be wound into a ball before you can begin knitting.

Yarn manufacturers (called spinners) wrap each ball with a paper band on which is printed a lot of necessary information. The ball band states the weight of the yarn and its composition. It will give instructions for the washing and ironing and will state the ideal range of needle sizes to be used with the yarn. The ball band also carries the shade number and dye lot number. It is important that you use yarn of the same dye lot for an entire project. Different dye lots vary subtly that may not be apparent when you are holding the two balls, but which will show as a variation in shade on the finished piece of knitting.

Always keep the ball band as a reference. The best way is to pin it to the gauge swatch (see page 17) and keep them together with any left over yarn and spare buttons or other trimmings. That way you can always check the washing instructions and also have materials for repairs.

the basics

Once you have mastered the basics of knitting, you can go on to develop your skills and start making more challenging projects.

Casting On

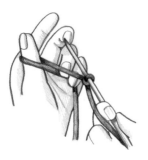

1 Make a slip knot 39in (1m) from the end of the yarn. Hold the needle in your right hand with the ball end of the yarn over your index finger. Wind the loose end of the yarn around your left thumb from front to back.

2 Insert the point of the needle under the first strand of yarn on your thumb.

3 With your right index finger, take the ball end of the yarn over the point of the needle.

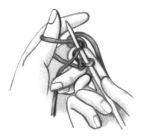

4 Pull a loop through to form the first stitch. Remove your left thumb from the yarn. Pull the loose end to secure the stitch. Repeat until all stitches have been cast on.

Knit Stitch

1 Hold the needle with the cast-on stitches in your left hand, with the loose yarn at the back of the work. Insert the right-hand needle from the left to right through the front of the first stitch on the left-hand needle.

2 Wind the yarn from left to right over the point of the right-hand needle.

3 Draw the yarn through the stitch, thus forming a new stitch on the right-hand needle.

4 Slip the original stitch off the left-hand needle, keeping the new stitch on the right-hand needle.

5 To knit a row, repeat steps 1 to 4 until all the stitches have been transferred from the left-hand needle to the right-hand needle. Turn the work, transferring the needle with the stitches to your left hand to work the next row.

Purl Stitch

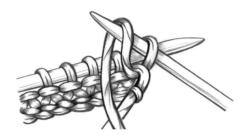

1 Hold the needle with the stitches in your left hand with the loose yarn at the front of the work. Insert the right-hand needle from right to left into the front of the front of the first stitch on the left-hand needle.

2 Wind the yarn from right to left over the point of the right-hand needle.

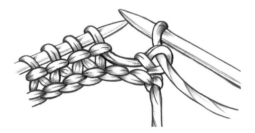

3 Draw the yarn through the stitch, thus forming a new stitch on the right-hand needle.

4 Slip the original stitch off the left-hand needle, keeping the new stitch on the right-hand needle.

5 To purl a row, repeat steps 1 to 4 until all the stitches have been transferred from the left-hand needle to the right-hand needle. Turn the work, transferring the needle with the stitches to your left hand to work the next row.

Increasing

The simplest method of increasing one stitch is to work into the front and back of the same stitch.

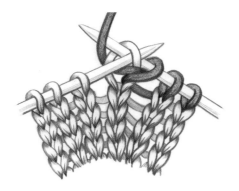

On a knit row, knit into the front of the stitch to be increased, then before slipping it off the needle, place the right-hand needle behind the left-hand needle and knit again into the back of the same stitch. Slip the original stitch off the left-hand needle.

On a purl row, purl into the front of the stitch to be increased, then before slipping it off the needle, purl again into the back of the same stitch. Slip the original stitch off the left-hand needle.

Decreasing

The simplest method of decreasing one stitch is to work two stitches together.

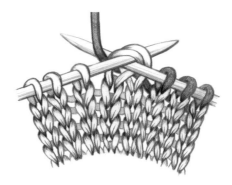

On a knit row, insert the right-hand needle from left to right through two stitches instead of one, then knit them together as one stitch. This is called knit two together (k2tog).

On a purl row, insert the right-hand needle from right to left through two stitches instead of one, then purl them together as one stitch. This is called purl two together (p2tog).

Binding Off

There is one simple, most commonly used method of securing stitches once you have finished a piece of knitting —binding off. The bind-off edge should always have the same "give" or elasticity as the fabric and you should always bind off in the stitch pattern used for the main fabric unless the pattern directs otherwise.

Knitwise

Knit two stitches. *Using the point of the left-hand needle, lift the first stitch on the right-hand needle over the second then drop it off the needle. Knit the next stitch and repeat from * until all stitches have been worked off the left-hand needle and only one stitch remains on the right-hand needle. Cut the yarn (leaving enough to sew in the end), thread the end through the stitch then slip it off the needle. Draw the yarn up firmly to fasten off.

Purlwise

Purl two stitches. *Using the point of the left-hand needle, lift the first stitch on the right-hand needle over the second and drop it off the needle. Purl the next stitch and repeat from * until all the stitches have been worked off the left-hand needle and only one stitch remains on the right-hand needle. Secure the last stitch as described for binding off knitwise.

The excitement of arriving at the last stage of your knitting can make you bind off without the same care that you have used in the rest of the work. You should take into account the part of the garment you are working on. If it is a neckband, you need to make sure that your bind-off edge is not too tight, preventing the neck from going over the wearer's head. If you are a tight knitter, you may need to bind off with a larger needle. Most neckbands or frontbands on a jacket or cardigan are worked in rib and should be bound off "ribwise" by knitting the knit stitches and purling the purl stitches as you bind off along the row. Lace stitches should also be bound off in pattern, slipping, making stitches, or decreasing as you go to make sure that the fabric doesn't widen or gather up.

Gauge (or tension)

The correct gauge (or tension) is the most important contribution to the successful knitting of a garment. The information under this heading given at the beginning of all patterns refers to the number of stitches required to fill a particular area; for example, a frequent gauge indication would be "22sts and 30 rows = 4in (10cms) square measured over stockinette stitch on size 6 (4mm) needles." This means that it is necessary to produce fabric made up of the proportion of stitches and rows as given in the gauge paragraph in order to obtain the correct measurements for the garment you intend to knit, regardless of the needles you use. The needle size indicated in the pattern is the one which most knitters will use to achieve this gauge, but it is the gauge that is important, not needle size.

The way to ensure that you do achieve the correct gauge is to work a gauge sample or swatch before starting the main part of the knitting. Although this may seem to be time wasting and a nuisance, it can save the enormous amount of time and aggravation that would result from having knitted a garment the wrong size.

Gauge Swatch

The instructions given in the gauge paragraph of a knitting pattern are either for working in stockinette stitch or in pattern stitch. If they are given in pattern stitch, it is necessary to work a multiple of stitches the same as the multiple required in the pattern. If in stockinette stitch, any number can be cast on, but whichever method is used there should always be at least 5in (12cm) wide. Work in pattern or stockinette stitch according to the wording of the gauge paragraph until the piece measures at least 4in (10cm) in depth. Break the yarn about 6in (15cm) from the work and thread this end through the stitches, then remove the knitting needle. Place a pin vertically into the fabric a few

stitches from the side edge. Measure 4in (10cm) carefully and insert a second pin. Count the stitches. If the number of stitches between the pins is less than that specified in the pattern (even by half a stitch) your garment will be too large. Use smaller needles and knit another gauge sample. If your sample has more stitches over 4in (10cm), the garment will be too small. Change to larger needles. Check the number of rows against the given gauge also.

It is most important to get the width measurement correct before starting to knit. Length measurements can usually be adjusted during the course of the knitting by adjusting the measurements to underarm or sleeve length, which is frequently given as a measurement and not in rows.

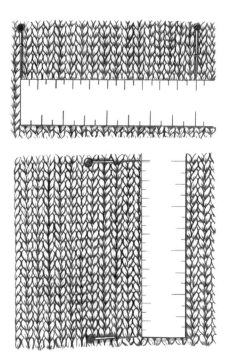

How to Read Charts

Charts are read exactly as the knitting is worked—from the bottom to the top. After the last row at the top has been worked, repeat the sequence from row 1.

Each symbol represents an instruction. Symbols have been designed to resemble the actual appearance of the knitting. This is more difficult to do with multicolor slip-stitch patterns, that have to be knitted before the mosaic effects become obvious.

Before starting to knit, look up all the symbols on your chosen chart so that you are familiar with the techniques involved. These may be shown with the pattern as a special abbreviation. The most common abbreviations that are not shown as special abbreviations will be given at the bottom of each page. Make sure you understand the difference between working similar symbols on a right-side and a wrong-side row. Before working a particular pattern, it is important to read the relevant information.

Each square represents a stitch and each horizontal line represents a row. Place a ruler above the line you are working and work the symbols one by one. If you are new to chart reading, try comparing the charted instructions with the written ones.

For knitters who wish to follow the written directions, it is still a good idea to look at the chart (where available) before starting, to see what the repeat looks like and how the pattern had been balanced.

Right-Side and Wrong-Side Rows

"Right-side rows" are rows where the right side of the fabric is facing you when you work, and "wrong-side rows" are rows where the wrong side is facing you when you work. Row numbers are shown at the side of the charts at the beginning of the row. Right-side rows are always read from right to left. Wrong-side rows are always read from left to right.

Symbols on charts are shown as they appear from the right side of the work. Therefore, a horizontal dash strands for a purl "bump" on the right side regardless of whether it was achieved by purling on a right-side row or knitting on a wrong-side row. To make things clearer, symbols for right-side rows are slightly darker than those for wrong-side rows.

Pattern Repeats and Multiples

The "Multiple" or repeat of the pattern is given with each set of instructions—for example "Multiple of 7 + 4". This means you can cast on any number of stitches which is a multiple of 7, plus 4 balancing stitches. For instance, 14 + 4, 21 + 4, 28 + 4, etc.

In the written instructions, the 7 stitches are shown in parentheses or brackets or follow an asterisk *, and these stitches are repeated across the row the required number of times. In charted instructions, the pattern repeat is contained between heavier vertical lines. The extra stitches not included in the pattern repeat are there to "balance" the row or make it symmetrical and are only worked once.

Some patterns require a foundation row that is worked once before commencing the pattern but does not form part of the repeat. On charts, this row is marked by a letter "F" and is separated from the pattern repeat by a heavier horizontal line.

stitch
gallery

Garter Stitch

Knit every row.

Stockinette Stitch

Any number of stitches.

1st row (right side): Knit.

2nd row: Purl.

Rep these 2 rows.

Reverse Stockinette Stitch

Any number of stitches.

1st row (right side): Purl.

2nd row: Knit.

Rep these 2 rows.

K1, P1, Rib

On an even number of sts:

*K1, p1; rep from * to end.

Rep this row.

On an odd number of sts:

1st row: K1, *p1, k1; rep from * to end.

2nd row: P1, *k1, p1; rep from * to end.

Rep these 2 rows.

K2, P2, Rib

Multiple of 4.
1st row: *K2, p2; rep from * to end.
Rep this row.

Multiple of 4 plus 2.
1st row: K2, *p2, k2; rep from * to end.
2nd row: P2, *k2, p2; rep from * to end.
Rep these 2 rows.

Linen Stitch

Multiple of 2.

1st row: *K1, yf, sl 1, yb*; rep from * to end.

2nd row: *P1, yb, sl 1, yf*; rep from * to end.

Rep these 2 rows.

Cartridge Stitch

Any number of stitches.

1st (right side), 3rd, 4th, and 6th rows: Knit.

2nd and 5th rows: Purl.

Rep these 6 rows.

Alternated Smooth Stitch and Tier

Any number of stitches.

1st (right side), 3rd, and 4th rows: Knit.

2nd row: Purl.

Rep these 4 rows.

Texture Stitch

Multiple of 2 + 1.

1st row (right side): Purl.

2nd row: K1, *yf, sl 1 purlwise, yb, k1; rep from * to end.

Rep these 2 rows.

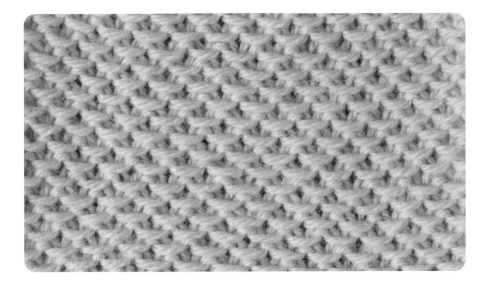

Loop Pattern

Multiple of 2 + 2.

1st row (right side): Knit.

2nd row: *K1, sl 1; rep from * to last 2 sts, k2.

3rd row: Knit.

4th row: K2, *sl 1, k1, rep from * to end.

Rep these 4 rows.

Herringbone I

Multiple of 2.

1st row: K2tog tbl dropping only first loop off left needle, *k2tog tbl (the remaining stitch and next stitch), again dropping only the first loop off the needle*, k1tbl.

2nd row: P2tog dropping only the first loop off left needle, *p2tog (the remaining stitch and next stitch), again dropping only first loop off needle*, p1.

Rep these 2 rows.

Gathered Stitch

Any number of stitches.

1st to 6th rows: Knit.

7th row: Knit into front and back of each st.

8th, 10th, and 12th rows: Purl.

9th and 11th rows: Knit.

13th row: K2tog to end.

Rep from 2nd row.

Pleat Pattern

Multiple of 5 + 1.

1st row (right side): K1B, *p1, k2, p1, k1B; rep from *.

2nd row: P1, *k1, p2, k1, p1; rep from *.

3rd row: K1B, *p4, k1B; rep from *.

4th row: P1, *k4, p1; rep from *.

Rep these 4 rows.

Whelk Pattern

Multiple of 4 + 3.

1st row (right side): K3, *sl 1 purlwise, k3; rep from * to end.

2nd row: K3, *yf, sl 1 purlwise, yb, k3; rep from * to end.

3rd row: K1, *sl 1 purlwise, k3; rep from * to last 2 sts, sl 1 purlwise, k1.

4th row: P1, sl 1 purlwise, *p3, sl 1 purlwise; rep from * to last st, p1.

Rep these 4 rows.

Bobble Stitch

Multiple of 12 + 11.

1st row: Knit.

2nd row: Purl.

3rd row: K5, *make 5 sts out of 1 st by knitting into front and back of next st twice, then into front again, turn, work 4 rows in St st (starting purl) on these 5 sts, with left-hand needle lift 2nd, 3rd, 4th and 5th sts over the first st (one bobble made), k11; rep from * to last 6 sts, work a bobble in next st, k5.

4th to 14th rows: Starting with a purl row work 11 rows in St st.

15th row (right side): K11, *work a bobble in next st, k11; rep from * to end.

16th to 26th rows: Work 11 rows in St st.

Repeat from 3rd row.

Fur Stitch

Multiple of 2 + 2.

1st row (wrong side): Knit.

2nd row: *K1, k1 keeping st on left-hand needle, bring yf, pass yarn over left thumb to make a loop (approx 1½in, 4cm), yb and knit this st again, slipping st off the needle, yo and pass the 2 sts just worked over this loop (1 loop made = ML); rep from * to last 2 sts, k2.

3rd row: Knit.

4th row: K2, *ML, k1; rep from * to end.

Rep these 4 rows.

Knitting Pattern 1

Multiple of 4 + 2.

1st row (right side): Edge st, *p1, k3; rep from * to last st, edge st.

2nd row: Edge st, p2 *k1, p3; rep from * to last 3 sts, k1, p1, edge st.

3rd row: Edge st, k2, *p1, k3; rep from * to last 3 sts, p1, k1, edge st.

4th row: Edge st, *k1, p3; rep from * to last st, edge st.

Rep these 4 rows.

This pattern can be used on either side.

Bowknot

Multiple of 10 + 7.

1st and 3rd rows (wrong side): Purl.

2nd, 4th, 6th, and 8th rows: Knit.

5th, 7th, and 9th rows: P6, *yb, sl 5 sts, yf, p5; rep from* to last st, p1.

10th row: K8, *make bowknot [slip right needle under 3 strands, knit next st pulling the loop through under the strands], k8, rep from * to end.

11th and 13th rows: Purl.

12th, 14th, 16th, and 18th rows: Knit.

15th, 17th, and 19th rows: P1, *yb, sl 5 sts, yf, p5; rep from * to last 6 sts, yb, sl 5 sts, p1.

Row 20: K3, *bowknot, k9; rep from * to last 4 sts, bowknot, k3.

Rep these 20 rows.

Ornamental Stitches

Multiple of 10 + 8.

1st, 3rd, and 5th rows: Knit.

2nd, 4th, and 6th rows: Purl.

7th row: K2, make daisy [insert needle in loop 3 rows below the 2nd st on left needle, draw up a loop, K2, draw 2nd loop through same st, k2, draw 3rd loop through same st], *k6, make daisy; rep from * to last 2 sts, k2.

8th row: P2, *[p2tog, p1] twice, p2tog, p5; rep from * to last 9 sts, [p2tog, p1] twice, p2tog, p1.

9th, 11th, and 13th rows: Knit.

10th, 12th, and 14th rows: Purl.

15th row: K7, *make daisy, k6; rep from * to last st, k1.

16th row: P2, *p5, [p2tog, p1] twice, p2tog; rep from * to last 6 sts, p6.

Rep these 16 rows.

Pleats

Multiple of 2 +1 + 2 sts each edge.

1st row (right side): Edge st, *k1, p1; rep from * to last 2 sts, k1, edge st.

2nd row: Edge st, p1, *k1, p1; rep from * to last st, edge st.

3rd , 5th , 7th & 9th row: Edge st, *k1, yf, sl 1 purlwise, yb; rep from * to last 2 sts, k1, edge st.

4th , 6th , 8th & 10th row: Edge st, *yf, slip 1 purlwise, yb, k1; rep from * to last 2 sts, yf, slip 1 purlwise, yb, edge st.

Rep these 10 rows.

Ribbed Extended Stitches

Multiple of 8 + 4 + 2 edge sts.

1st row (right side): Edge st, *p4, k4 (winding yarn round needle three times for each st)*; rep from * to last st, edge st.

2nd and 4th rows: Edge st, k4, *yf, slip 4 sts purlwise dropping extra loops off needle, yb, k4; rep from * to last st, edge st.

3rd row: Edge st, *p4, yb, slip 4 sts knitwise, yf; rep from * to last st, edge st.

Rep these 4 rows.

Vertical Bar Lines

Multiple of 4 + 2.

1st row (right side): P2, *k2, p2; rep from * to end.

2nd row: K2, *keeping yarn to the back slip next 2 sts purlwise, k2; rep from * to end.

Rep these 2 rows.

Open-Work Mullions

Multiple of 5 + 1.

1st row (right side): P1, *k4, p1; rep from * to end.

2nd row: K1, *k twice into st below st on needle, k2tog, k into st below st on needle, p1; rep from * to end.

Rep these 2 rows.

Knitting Pattern 11

Multiple of 18 + 2 edge sts.

1st row: Edge st, *p4, k4, p1, k4, p1, k4; rep from * to last st, edge st.

2nd row: Edge st, *k1, p4, k4, p4, k1, p4; rep from * to last st, edge st.

3rd row: Edge st, k5, *p1, k10, p1, k6; rep from * to last 14 sts, p1, k10, p1, k1, edge st.

4th row: Edge st, p2, *k1, p8, k1, p8; rep from * to last 17 sts, k1, p8, k1, p6, edge st.

5th row: Edge st, k7 *p1, k6, p1, k10; rep from * to last 12 sts, p1, k6, p1, k3, edge st.

6th row: Edge st, *p4, k1, p4, k1, p4, k4*; rep from * to last st, edge st.

7th row: Edge st, *k4, p1, k4, p4, k4, p1; rep from * to last st, edge st.

8th row: Edge st, p1 *k1, p10, k1, p6; rep from * to last 18 sts, k1, p10, k1, p5, edge st.

9th row: Edge st, k6 *p1, k8, p1, k8; rep from * to last 13 sts, p1, k8, p1, k2, edge st.

10th row: Edge st, p3 *k1, p6, k1, p10; rep from * to last 16 sts, k1, p6, k1, p7, edge st.

Rep these 10 rows.

Labyrinth

Panel of 40 sts.

1st & 3rd rows (right side): K2, p2, k2, p2, k2, p8, k2, p2, k2, p16.

2nd & even rows: Knit all k sts and purl all p sts.

5th & 7th rows: K2, p2 (3 times), k8, p2, k2, p2, k14.

9th & 11th rows: K2, p2 (4 times), p6, k2, p2, k2, p12.

13th & 15th rows: K2, p2 (4 times), k8, p2, k2, p2, k10.

17th & 19th rows: K2, p2 (4 times), p10, k2, p2, k2, p8.

21st & 23rd rows: K2, p2 (4 times), k12, p2, k2, p2, k6.

25th & 27th rows: K6, p2, k2, p2, k2, p12, k2, p2, k2, p2, k2, p4.

29th & 31st rows: P8, k2, p2, k2, p2, k12, p2, k2 (3 times).

33rd & 35th rows: K10, p2, k2, p2, k2, p12, k2, p2, k2, p2, k2.

37th & 39th rows: P12, k2, p2, k16, p2, k12, p2, k2.

41st & 43rd rows: K14, p2, k2, p16, k2, p2, k2.

45th & 47th rows: P12, k2, p2, k20, p2, k2.

48th row: As row 2.

Repeat these 48 rows.

Plain Diamonds

Multiple of 9.

1st row (right side): K4, *p1, k8; rep from * to last 5 sts, p1, k4.

2nd row: P3, *k3, p6; rep from * to last 6 sts, k3, p3.

3rd row: K2, *p5, k4; rep from * to last 7 sts, p5, k2.

4th row: P1, *k7, p2; rep from * to last 8 sts, k7, p1.

5th row: Purl.

6th row: As 4th row.

7th row: As 3rd row.

8th row: As 2nd row.

Rep these 8 rows.

Experiment with different stitches to give a totally new element to a favorite design or pattern.

Supple Rib

Multiple of 3 + 1.

1st row (right side): K1, *knit the next st but do not slip it off the left-hand needle, then purl the same st and the next st tog, k1; rep from * to end.

2nd row: Purl.

Rep these 2 rows.

Dot Stitch

Multiple of 4 + 3.

1st row (right side): K1, *p1, k3; rep from * to last 2 sts, p1, k1.

2nd row: Purl.

3rd row: *K3, p1; rep from * to last 3 sts, k3.

4th row: Purl.

Rep these 4 rows.

Embossed Diamonds

Multiple of 10 + 3.

1st row (right side): P1, k1, p1, *[k3, p1] twice, k1, p1; rep from * to end.

2nd row: P1, k1, *p3, k1, p1, k1, p3, k1; rep from * to last st, p1.

3rd row: K4, *[p1, k1] twice, p1, k5; rep from * to last 9 sts, [p1, k1] twice, p1, k4.

4th row: P3, *[k1, p1] 3 times, k1, p3; rep from * to end.

5th row: As 3rd row.

6th row: As 2nd row.

7th row: As 1st row.

8th row: P1, k1, p1, *k1, p5, [k1, p1] twice; rep from * to end.

9th row: [P1, k1] twice, *p1, k3, [p1, k1] 3 times; rep from * to last 9 sts, p1, k3, [p1, k1] twice, p1.

10th row: As 8th row.

Rep these 10 rows.

Farrow Rib

Multiple of 3 + 1.

1st row (right side): *K2, p1; rep from * to last st, k1.

2nd row: P1, *k2, p1; rep from * to end.

Rep these 2 rows.

Look at the reverse side of the stitch swatch too; often it can be more pleasing than the front.

Cross Motif Pattern 1

Multiple of 12.

1st row (right side): P1, k10, *p2, k10; rep from * to last st, p1.

2nd row: K1, p10, *k2, p10; rep from * to last st, k1.

Rep the last 2 rows once more.

5th row: P3, k6, *p6, k6; rep from * to last 3 sts, p3.

6th row: K3, p6, *k6, p6; rep from * to last 3 sts, k3.

7th row: As 1st row.

8th row: As 2nd row.

Rep the last 2 rows once more.

11th row: Knit.

12th row: Purl.

13th row: K5, p2, *k10, p2; rep from * to last 5 sts, k5.

14th row: P5, k2, *p10, k2; rep from * to last 5 sts, p5.

Rep the last 2 rows once more.

17th row: K3, p6, *k6, p6; rep from * to last 3 sts, k3.

18th row: P3, k6, *p6, k6; rep from * to last 3 sts, p3.

19th row: K5, p2, *k10, p2; rep from * to last 5 sts, k5.

20th row: P5, k2, *p10, k2; rep from * to last 5 sts, p5.

Rep the last 2 rows once more.

23rd row: Knit.

24th row: Purl.

Rep these 24 rows.

Box Stitch

Multiple of 4 + 2.

1st row: K2, *p2, k2; rep from * to end.

2nd row: P2, *k2, p2; rep from * to end.

3rd row: As 2nd row.

4th row: As 1st row.

Rep these 4 rows.

Moss Stitch Parallelograms

Multiple of 10.

1st row (right side): *K5, [p1, k1] twice, p1; rep from * to end.

2nd row: [P1, k1] 3 times, *p5, [k1, p1] twice, k1; rep from * to last 4 sts, p4.

3rd row: K3, *[p1, k1] twice, p1, k5; rep from * to last 7 sts, [p1, k1] twice, p1, k2.

4th row: P3, *[k1, p1] twice, k1, p5; rep from * to last 7 sts, [k1, p1] twice, k1, p2.

5th row: [K1, p1] 3 times, *k5, [p1, k1] twice, p1; rep from * to last 4 sts, k4.

6th row: Purl.

Rep these 6 rows.

Oblique Rib

Multiple of 4.

1st row (right side): *K2, p2; rep from * to end.

2nd row: K1, *p2, k2; rep from * to last 3 sts, p2, k1.

3rd row: *P2, k2; rep from * to end.

4th row: P1, *k2, p2; rep from * to last 3 sts, k2, p1.

Rep these 4 rows.

Woven Horizontal Herringbone

Multiple of 4.

1st row (right side): K3, *yf, sl 2, yb, k2; rep from * to last st, k1.

2nd row: P2, *yb, sl 2, yf, p2; rep from * to last 2 sts, p2.

3rd row: K1, yf, sl 2, yb, *k2, yf, sl 2, yb; rep from * to last st, k1.

4th row: P4, *yb, sl 2, yf, p2; rep from * to end.

Rep the last 4 rows twice more.

13th row: As 3rd row.

14th row: As 2nd row.

Rep these 14 rows.

Lizard Lattice

Multiple of 6 + 3.

Work 4 rows in st st, starting knit (1st row is right side).

5th row: P3, *k3, p3; rep from * to end.

6th row: Purl.

Rep the last 2 rows once more, then 5th row again.

Work 4 rows in st st, starting purl.

14th row: P3, *k3, p3; rep from * to end.

Rep these 14 rows.

Have a good range of needle sizes to hand to experiment readily.

Moss Stitch Triangles

Multiple of 8.

1st row (right side): *P1, k7; rep from * to end.

2nd row: P6, *k1, p7; rep from * to last 2 sts, k1, p1.

3rd row: *P1, k1, p1, k5; rep from * to end.

4th row: P4, *k1, p1, k1, p5; rep from * to last 4 sts, [k1, p1] twice.

5th row: *[P1, k1] twice, p1, k3; rep from * to end.

6th row: P2, *[k1, p1] twice, k1, p3; rep from * to last 6 sts, [k1, p1] 3 times.

7th row: *P1, k1; rep from * to end.

8th row: As 6th row.

9th row: As 5th row.

10th row: As 4th row.

11th row: As 3rd row.

12th row: As 2nd row.

Rep these 12 rows.

Double Moss Stitch

Multiple of 2 + 1.

1st row: K1, *p1, k1; rep from * to end.

2nd row: P1, *k1, p1; rep from * to end.

3rd row: As 2nd row.

4th row: As 1st row.

Rep these 4 rows.

Pyramids 1

Multiple of 15 + 7.

1st row (right side): *P1, [KB1] 5 times, p1, k8; rep from * to last 7 sts, p1, [KB1] 5 times, p1.

2nd row: *K1, [PB1] 5 times, k1, p8; rep from * to last 7 sts, k1, [PB1] 5 times, k1.

3rd row: P1, *[KB1] 5 times, p10; rep from * to last 6 sts, [KB1] 5 times, p1.

4th row: K1, *[PB1] 5 times, k10; rep from * to last 6 sts, [PB1] 5 times, k1.

5th row: P2, *[KB1] 3 times, p3, k6, p3; rep from * to last 5 sts, [KB1] 3 times, p2.

6th row: K2, *[PB1] 3 times, k3, p6, k3; rep from * to last 5 sts, [PB1] 3 times, k2.

7th row: P2, *[KB1] 3 times, p12; rep from * to last 5 sts, [KB1] 3 times, p2.

8th row: K2, *[PB1] 3 times, k12; rep from * to last 5 sts, [PB1] 3 times, k2.

9th row: P3, *KB1, p5, k4, p5; rep from * to last 4 sts, KB1, p3.

10th row: K3, *PB1, k5, p4, k5; rep from * to last 4 sts, PB1, k3.

11th row: P3, *KB1, p14; rep from * to last 4 sts, KB1, p3.

12th row: K3, *PB1, k14; rep from * to last 4 sts, PB1, k3.

Rep these 12 rows.

Little Birds

Multiple of 14 + 8.

1st row (right side): Knit.

2nd row: Purl.

3rd row: K10, *sl 2 purlwise, k12; rep from * to last 12 sts, sl 2 purlwise, k10.

4th row: P10, *sl 2 purlwise, p12; rep from * to last 12 sts, sl 2 purlwise, p10.

5th row: K8, *C3R, C3L, k8; rep from * to end.

6th row: Purl.

Rep 1st and 2nd rows once.

9th row: K3, *sl 2, k12; rep from * to last 5 sts, sl 2, k3.

10th row: P3, *sl 2, p12; rep from * to last 5 sts, sl 2, p3.

11th row: K1, *C3R, C3L, k8; rep from * to last 7 sts, C3R, C3L, k1.

12th row: Purl.

Rep these 12 rows.

Chevron Stripes

Multiple of 18 + 9.

1st row (right side): P4, k1, p4, *k4, p1, k4, p4, k1, p4; rep from * to end.

2nd row: K3, *p3, k3; rep from * to end.

3rd row: P2, k5, p2, *k2, p5, k2, p2, k5, p2; rep from * to end.

4th row: K1, p7, k1, *p1, k7, p1, k1, p7, k1; rep from * to end.

5th row: K4, p1, k4, *p4, k1, p4, k4, p1, k4; rep from * to end.

6th row: P3, *k3, p3; rep from * to end.

7th row: K2, p5, k2, *p2, k5, p2, k2, p5, k2; rep from * to end.

8th row: P1, k7, p1, *k1, p7, k1, p1, k7, p1; rep from * to end.

Rep these 8 rows.

Moss Stitch 1

Multiple of 2 + 1.

1st row: K1, *p1, k1; rep from * to end.

Rep this row.

Select several stitch swatches that may work together; they may compliment one another or contrast, think scale, shape or type.

Stockinette Stitch Triangles

Multiple of 5.

1st row (right side): Knit.

2nd row: *K1, p4; rep from * to end.

3rd row: *K3, p2; rep from * to end.

4th row: *K3, p2; rep from * to end.

5th row: *K1, p4; rep from * to end.

6th row: Knit.

Rep these 6 rows.

Moss Stitch Squares

Multiple of 12 + 3.

1st row (right side): Knit.

2nd row: Purl.

3rd row: K4, *[p1, k1] 3 times, p1, k5; rep from * to last 11 sts, [p1, k1] 3 times, p1, k4.

4th row: P3, *[k1, p1] 4 times, k1, p3; rep from * to end.

5th row: K4, *p1, k5; rep from * to last 5 sts, p1, k4.

6th row: P3, *k1, p7, k1, p3; rep from * to end.

Rep the last 2 rows twice more, then the 5th row again.

12th row: As 4th row.

13th row: As 3rd row.

14th row: Purl.

Rep these 14 rows.

Double Rice Stitch 1

Multiple of 2 + 1.

1st row (wrong side): P1, *KB1, p1; rep from * to end.

2nd row: Knit.

3rd row: *KB1, p1; rep from * to last st, KB1.

4th row: Knit.

Rep these 4 rows.

Open Chain Ribbing

Multiple of 6 + 2.

1st row (wrong side): K2, *p4, k2; rep from * to end.

2nd row: P2, *k2tog, [yo] twice, sl 1, k1, psso, p2; rep from * to end.

3rd row: K2, *p1, purl into front of first yo, purl into back of 2nd yo, p1, k2; rep from * to end.

4th row: P2, *yon, sl 1, k1, psso, k2tog, yfrn, p2; rep from * to end.

Rep these 4 rows.

Moss Stitch Diagonal

Multiple of 8 + 3.

1st row (right side): K4, *p1, k1, p1, k5; rep from * to last 7 sts, p1, k1, p1, k4.

2nd row: P3, *[k1, p1] twice, k1, p3; rep from * to end.

3rd row: K2, *p1, k1, p1, k5; rep from * to last st, p1.

4th row: P1, k1, *p3, [k1, p1] twice, k1; rep from * to last st, p1.

5th row: *P1, k1, p1, k5; rep from * to last 3 sts, p1, k1, p1.

6th row: *[P1, k1] twice, p3, k1; rep from * to last 3 sts, p1, k1, p1.

7th row: P1, *k5, p1, k1, p1; rep from * to last 2 sts, k2.

8th row: [P1, k1] 3 times, *p3, [k1, p1] twice, k1; rep from * to last 5 sts, p3, k1, p1.

Rep these 8 rows.

Checkerboard

Multiple of 8 + 4.

1st row: K4, *p4, k4; rep from * to end.

2nd row: P4, *k4, p4; rep from * to end.

Rep the last 2 rows once more.

5th row: As 2nd row.

6th row: As 1st row.

Rep the last 2 rows once more.

Rep these 8 rows.

Hexagon Stitch

Multiple of 10 + 1.

1st row (right side): Knit.

2nd row: Purl.

3rd row: K4, *p1, k1, p1, k7; rep from * to last 7 sts, p1, k1, p1, k4.

4th row: P3, *[k1, p1] twice, k1, p5; rep from * to last 8 sts, [k1, p1] twice, k1, p3.

5th row: K2, *[p1, k1] 3 times, p1, k3; rep from * to last 9 sts, [p1, k1] 3 times, p1, k2.

Rep the last 2 rows once more.

8th row: As 4th row.

9th row: As 3rd row.

10th row: Purl.

11th row: Knit.

12th row: Purl.

13th row: K1, p1, *k7, p1, k1, p1; rep from * to last 9 sts, k7, p1, k1.

14th row: K1, p1, k1, *p5, [k1, p1] twice, k1; rep from * to last 8 sts, p5, k1, p1, k1.

15th row: [K1, p1] twice, *k3, [p1, k1] 3 times, p1; rep from * to last 7 sts, k3, [p1, k1] twice.

Rep the last 2 rows once more.

18th row: As 14th row.

19th row: As 13th row.

20th row: Purl.

Rep these 20 rows.

Woven Stitch 1

Multiple of 2 + 1.

1st row (right side): K1, *yf, sl 1, yb, k1; rep from * to
end.

2nd row: Purl.

3rd row: K2, *yf, sl 1, yb, k1; rep from * to last st, k1.

4th row: Purl.

Rep these 4 rows.

Alternate Bobble Stripe

Multiple of 10 + 5.

1st row (right side): P2, k1, *p4, k1; rep from * to last 2 sts, p2.

2nd row: K2, p1, *k4, p1; rep from * to last 2 sts, k2.

3rd row: P2, *MB (Make bobble) as follows: work [k1, p1, k1, p1, k1] into the next st, turn and k5, turn and k5tog (bobble completed), p4, k1, p4; rep from * to last 3 sts, MB, p2.

4th row: As 2nd row.

Rep the last 4 rows 4 times more.

21st row: As 1st row.

22nd row: As 2nd row.

23rd row: P2, *k1, p4, MB, p4; rep from * to last 3 sts, k1, p2.

24th row: As 2nd row.

Rep the last 4 rows 4 times more.

Rep these 40 rows.

Moss Stitch Panes

Multiple of 10 + 3.

1st row (right side): P1, *k1, p1; rep from * to end.

2nd row: P1, *k1, p1; rep from * to end.

3rd row: P1, k1, p1, *k7, p1, k1, p1; rep from * to end.

4th row: P1, k1, p9, *k1, p9; rep from * to last 2 sts, k1, p1.

Rep the last 2 rows 3 times more.

Rep these 10 rows.

When I want to do a swatch quickly, I use the thumb method to cast on as it is so very easy and convenient, especially if travelling. It also gives a neat firm edge without having to knit into the back of the stitches on the first row.

Diagonal Garter Ribs

Multiple of 5 + 2.

1st and every alt row (right side): Knit.

2nd row: *P2, k3; rep from * to last 2 sts, p2.

4th row: K1, *p2, k3; rep from * to last st, p1.

6th row: K2, *p2, k3; rep from * to end.

8th row: *K3, p2; rep from * to last 2 sts, k2.

10th row: P1, *k3, p2; rep from * to last st, k1.

Rep these 10 rows.

Seed Stitch Checks

Multiple of 10 + 5.

1st row (right side): K5, *[p1, k1] twice, p1, k5; rep from * to end.

2nd row: P6, *k1, p1, k1, p7; rep from * to last 9 sts, k1, p1, k1, p6.

Rep the last 2 rows once more, then the 1st row again.

6th row: *[K1, p1] twice, k1, p5; rep from * to last 5 sts, [k1, p1] twice, k1.

7th row: [K1, p1] twice, *k7, p1, k1, p1; rep from * to last st, k1.

Rep the last 2 rows once more, then the 6th row again.

Rep these 10 rows.

Top Hat Pattern

Multiple of 6 + 4.

1st row (right side): K4, *p2, k4; rep from * to end.

2nd row: P4, *k2, p4; rep from * to end.

Rep the last 2 rows once more.

5th row: P1, k2, *p4, k2; rep from * to last st, p1.

6th row: K1, p2, *k4, p2; rep from * to last st, k1.

Rep the last 2 rows once more.

9th row: Purl.

10th row: Knit.

Rep these 10 rows.

Beaded Rib

Multiple of 5 + 2.

1st row (right side): P2, *k1, p1, k1, p2; rep from * to end.

2nd row: K2, *p3, k2; rep from * to end.

Rep these 2 rows.

Vertical Zigzag Moss Stitch

Multiple of 7.

1st row (right side): *P1, k1, p1, k4; rep from * to end.

2nd row: *P4, k1, p1, k1; rep from * to end.

3rd row: *[K1, p1] twice, k3; rep from * to end.

4th row: *P3, [k1, p1] twice; rep from * to end.

5th row: K2, p1, k1, p1, *k4, p1, k1, p1; rep from * to last 2 sts, k2.

6th row: P2, k1, p1, k1, *p4, k1, p1, k1; rep from * to last 2 sts, p2.

7th row: K3, p1, k1, p1, *k4, p1, k1, p1; rep from * to last st, k1.

8th row: [P1, k1] twice, *p4, k1, p1, k1; rep from * to last 3 sts, p3.

9th row: *K4, p1, k1, p1; rep from * to end.

10th row: *K1, p1, k1, p4; rep from * to end.

11th and 12th rows: As 7th and 8th rows.

13th and 14th rows: As 5th and 6th rows.

15th and 16th rows: As 3rd and 4th rows.

Rep these 16 rows.

Double Woven Stitch 1

Multiple of 4.

1st row (right side): K3, *yf, sl 2, yb, k2; rep from * to last st, k1.

2nd row: Purl.

3rd row: K1, *yf, sl 2, yb, k2; rep from * to last 3 sts, yf, sl 2, yb, k1.

4th row: Purl.

Rep these 4 rows.

Maze Pattern

Multiple of 13.

1st row (right side): Knit.

2nd row: Purl.

3rd row: Knit.

4th row: P1, k11, *p2, k11; rep from * to last st, p1.

5th row: K1, p11, *k2, p11; rep from * to last st, k1.

6th row: As 4th row.

7th row: K1, p2, k7, p2, *k2, p2, k7, p2; rep from * to last st, k1.

8th row: P1, k2, p7, k2, *p2, k2, p7, k2; rep from * to last st, p1.

9th row: As 7th row.

10th row: P1, k2, p2, k3, *[p2, k2] twice, p2, k3; rep from * to last 5 sts, p2, k2, p1.

11th row: K1, p2, k2, p3, *[k2, p2] twice, k2, p3; rep from * to last 5 sts, k2, p2, k1.

Rep the last 2 rows once more.

14th row: As 8th row.

15th row: As 7th row.

16th row: As 8th row.

17th row: As 5th row.

18th row: As 4th row.

19th row: As 5th row.

20th row: As 2nd row.

Rep these 20 rows.

Double Parallelogram Stitch

Multiple of 10.

1st row (right side): *P5, k5; rep from * to end.

2nd row: K1, *p5, k5; rep from * to last 9 sts, p5, k4.

3rd row: P3, *k5, p5; rep from * to last 7 sts, k5, p2.

4th row: K3, *p5, k5; rep from * to last 7 sts, p5, k2.

5th row: P1, *k5, p5; rep from * to last 9 sts, k5, p4.

6th row: P4, *k5, p5; rep from * to last 6 sts, k5, p1.

7th row: K2, *p5, k5; rep from * to last 8 sts, p5, k3.

8th row: P2, *k5, p5; rep from * to last 8 sts, k5, p3.

9th row: K4, *p5, k5; rep from * to last 6 sts, p5, k1.

10th row: *K5, p5; rep from * to end.

Rep these 10 rows.

2-Stitch Ribs 1

Multiple of 4 + 2.

1st row: K2, *p2, k2; rep from * to end.

Rep this row.

Introducing stripes into your stitch—regular, irregular, colorful, tonal, or self-colored—is an easy way to add color and texture to your knitting. Narrow, or broad, textured or smooth, the striping possibilities are endless.

Double Signal Check

Multiple of 18 + 9.

1st row (right side): K1, p7, k1, *p1, k7, p1, k1, p7, k1; rep from * to end.

2nd row: P2, k5, p2, *k2, p5, k2, p2, k5, p2; rep from * to end.

3rd row: K3, *p3, k3; rep from * to end.

4th row: P4, k1, p4, *k4, p1, k4, p4, k1, p4; rep from * to end.

5th row: P1, k7, p1, *k1, p7, k1, p1, k7, p1; rep from * to end.

6th row: K2, p5, k2, *p2, k5, p2, k2, p5, k2; rep from * to end.

7th row: P3, *k3, p3; rep from * to end.

8th row: K4, p1, k4, *p4, k1, p4, k4, p1, k4; rep from * to end.

Rep these 8 rows.

Eyelet Mock Cable Ribbing

Multiple of 5 + 2.

1st row (right side): P2, *sl 1, k2, psso, p2; rep from * to end.

2nd row: K2, *p1, yrn, p1, k2; rep from * to end.

3rd row: P2, *k3, p2; rep from * to end.

4th row: K2, *p3, k2; rep from * to end.

Rep these 4 rows.

King Charles Brocade

Multiple of 12 + 1.

1st row (right side): K1, *p1, k9, p1, k1; rep from * to end.

2nd row: K1, p1, k1, *p7, [k1, p1] twice, k1; rep from * to last 10 sts, p7, k1, p1, k1.

3rd row: [K1, p1] twice, *k5, [p1, k1] 3 times, p1; rep from * to last 9 sts, k5, [p1, k1] twice.

4th row: P2, *k1, p1, k1, p3; rep from * to last 5 sts, k1, p1, k1, p2.

5th row: K3, *[p1, k1] 3 times, p1, k5; rep from * to last 10 sts, [p1, k1] 3 times, p1, k3.

6th row: P4, *[k1, p1] twice, k1, p7; rep from * to last 9 sts, [k1, p1] twice, k1, p4.

7th row: K5, *p1, k1, p1, k9; rep from * to last 8 sts, p1, k1, p1, k5.

8th row: As 6th row.

9th row: As 5th row.

10th row: As 4th row.

11th row: As 3rd row.

12th row: As 2nd row.

Rep these 12 rows.

Garter Stitch Triangles

Multiple of 8 +1.

1st row (right side): P1, *k7, p1; rep from * to end.

2nd row and every alt row: Purl.

3rd row: P2, *k5, p3; rep from * to last 7 sts, k5, p2.

5th row: P3, *k3, p5; rep from * to last 6 sts, k3, p3.

7th row: P4, *k1, p7; rep from * to last 5 sts, k1, p4.

9th row: K4, *p1, k7; rep from * to last 5 sts, p1, k4.

11th row: K3, *p3, k5; rep from * to last 6 sts, p3, k3.

13th row: K2, *p5, k3; rep from * to last 7 sts; p5, k2.

15th row: K1, *p7, k1; rep from * to end.

16th row: Purl.

Rep these 16 rows.

Diagonals 1

Multiple of 8 + 6.

1st row (right side): P3, *k5, p3; rep from * to last 3 sts, k3.

2nd row: P4, *k3, p5; rep from * to last 2 sts, k2.

3rd row: P1, k5, *p3, k5; rep from * to end.

4th row: K1, p5, *k3, p5; rep from * to end.

5th row: K4, *p3, k5; rep from * to last 2 sts, p2.

6th row: K3, *p5, k3; rep from * to last 3 sts, p3.

7th row: K2, p3, *k5, p3; rep from * to last st, k1.

8th row: P2, k3, *p5, k3; rep from * to last st, p1.

Rep these 8 rows.

Diamond and Block

Multiple of 14 + 5.

1st row (right side): P5, *k4, p1, k4, p5; rep from * to end.

2nd row: K5, *p3, k3, p3, k5; rep from * to end.

3rd row: K7, p5, *k9, p5; rep from * to last 7 sts, k7.

4th row: P6, k7, *p7, k7; rep from * to last 6 sts, p6.

5th row: K5, *p9, k5; rep from * to end.

6th row: As 4th row.

7th row: As 3rd row.

8th row: As 2nd row.

Rep these 8 rows.

If you need to select a needle size for an unknown yarn, double your yarn and thread it through the closest-sized hole on your needle gauge. The hole which it fits through the neatest (neither tight nor with gaping spaces around the yarn) is the best needle size for your first swatch.

Divided Triangles

Multiple of 14 + 1.

1st row (wrong side): Knit.

2nd row: Knit.

3rd row: K1, *p13, k1; rep from * to end.

4th row: K1, *p1, k11, p1, k1; rep from * to end.

5th row: P1, *k2, p9, k2, p1; rep from * to end.

6th row: K1, *p3, k7, p3, k1; rep from * to end.

7th row: P1, *k4, p5, k4, p1; rep from * to end.

8th row: K1, *p5, k3, p5, k1; rep from * to end.

9th row: P1, *[k6, p1] twice; rep from * to end.

10th and 11th rows: Purl.

12th row: K7, p1, *k13, p1; rep from * to last 7 sts, k7.

13th row: P6, k1, p1, k1, *p11, k1, p1, k1; rep from * to last 6 sts, p6.

14th row: K5, p2, k1, p2, *k9, p2, k1, p2; rep from * to last 5 sts, k5.

15th row: P4, k3, p1, k3, *p7, k3, p1, k3; rep from * to last 4 sts, p4.

16th row: K3, p4, k1, p4, *k5, p4, k1, p4; rep from * to last 3 sts, k3.

17th row: P2, k5, p1, k5, *p3, k5, p1, k5; rep from * to last 2 sts, p2.

18th row: K1, *p6, k1; rep from * to end.

Rep these 18 rows.

Rib Checks

Multiple of 10 + 5.

1st row (right side): P5, *[KB1, p1] twice, KB1, p5; rep from * to end.

2nd row: K5, *[PB1, k1] twice, PB1, k5; rep from * to end.

Rep the last 2 rows once more, then the 1st row again.

6th row: [PB1, k1] twice, PB1, *k5, [PB1, k1] twice, PB1; rep from * to end.

7th row: [KB1, p1] twice, KB1, *p5, [KB1, p1] twice, KB1; rep from * to end.

Rep the last 2 rows once more, then the 6th row again.

Rep these 10 rows.

Diamond and Lozenge Pattern 1

Multiple of 12.

1st row (right side): *K6, p6; rep from * to end.

2nd row: *K6, p6; rep from * to end.

3rd and 4th rows: *P1, k5, p5, k1; rep from * to end.

5th and 6th rows: K1, p1, k4, p4, *[k1, p1] twice, k4, p4; rep from * to last 2 sts, k1, p1.

7th and 8th rows: P1, k1, p1, k3, p3, *[k1, p1] 3 times, k3, p3; rep from * to last 3 sts, k1, p1, k1.

9th and 10th rows: [K1, p1] twice, k2, p2, *[k1, p1] 4 times, k2, p2; rep from * to last 4 sts, [k1, p1] twice.

11th and 12th rows: *P1, k1; rep from * to end.

13th and 14th rows: *K1, p1; rep from * to end.

15th and 16th rows: [P1, k1] twice, p2, k2, *[p1, k1] 4 times, p2, k2; rep from * to last 4 sts, [p1, k1] twice.

17th and 18th rows: K1, p1, k1, p3, k3, *[p1, k1] 3 times, p3, k3; rep from * to last 3 sts, p1, k1, p1.

19th and 20th rows: P1, k1, p4, k4, *[p1, k1] twice, p4, k4; rep from * to last 2 sts, p1, k1.

21st and 22nd rows: *K1, p5, k5, p1; rep from * to end.

23rd and 24th rows: *P6, k6; rep from * to end.

25th and 26th rows: *P5, k1, p1, k5; rep from * to end.

27th and 28th rows: *P4, [k1, p1] twice, k4; rep from * to end.

29th and 30th rows: *P3, [k1, p1] 3 times, k3; rep from * to end.

31st and 32nd rows: *P2, [k1, p1] 4 times, k2; rep from * to end.

33rd and 34th rows: As 11th and 12th rows.

35th and 36th rows: As 13th and 14th rows.

37th and 38th rows: *K2, [p1, k1] 4 times, p2; rep from * to end.

39th and 40th rows: *K3, [p1, k1] 3 times, p3; rep from * to end.

41st and 42nd rows: *K4, [p1, k1] twice, p4; rep from * to end.

43rd and 44th rows: *K5, p1, k1, p5; rep from * to end.
Rep these 44 rows.

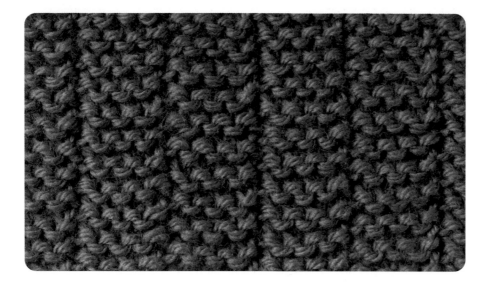

4-Stitch Ribs

Multiple of 8 + 4.

1st row: K4, *p4, k4; rep from * to end.

Rep this row.

There are myriad ways of using up your yarn stash. Use them for mitten cuffs, decorative ends on scarves, Fair Isle bands, wristwarmers, or even toys.

Purl Triangles

Multiple of 8 + 1.

1st row (right side): K1, *p7, k1; rep from * to end.

2nd row: P1, *k7, p1; rep from * to end.

3rd row: K2, *p5, k3; rep from * to last 7 sts, p5, k2.

4th row: P2, *k5, p3; rep from * to last 7 sts, k5, p2.

5th row: K3, *p3, k5; rep from * to last 6 sts, p3, k3.

6th row: P3, *k3, p5; rep from * to last 6 sts, k3, p3.

7th row: K4, *p1, k7; rep from * to last 5 sts, p1, k4.

8th row: P4, *k1, p7; rep from * to last 5 sts, k1, p4.

9th row: As 8th row.

10th row: As 7th row.

11th row: As 6th row.

12th row: As 5th row.

13th row: As 4th row.

14th row: As 3rd row.

15th row: As 2nd row.

16th row: K1, *p7, k1; rep from * to end.

Rep these 16 rows.

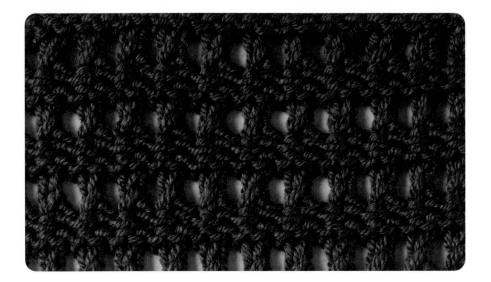

Open Check Stitch

Multiple of 2.

1st row (right side): Purl.

2nd row: Knit.

3rd row: K2, *sl 1, k1; rep from * to end.

4th row: *K1, yf, sl 1, yb; rep from * to last 2 sts, k2.

5th row: K1, *yo, k2tog; rep from * to last st, k1.

6th row: Purl.

Rep these 6 rows.

Textured Triangle Stack

Multiple of 10 + 1.

1st row (right side): P5, *k1, p9; rep from * to last 6 sts, k1, p5.

2nd row: K5, *p1, k9; rep from * to last 6 sts, p1, k5.

3rd row: P4, *k3, p7; rep from * to last 7 sts, p3, k4.

4th row: K4, *p3, k7; rep from * to last 7 sts, k3, p4.

5th row: P3, *k5, p5; rep from * to last 8 sts, k5, p3.

6th row: K3, *p5, k5; rep from * to last 8 sts, p5, k3.

7th row: P2, *k7, p3; rep from * to last 9 sts, k7, p2.

8th row: K2, *p7, k3; rep from * to last 9 sts, p7, k2.

9th row: P1, *k9, p1; rep from * to end.

10th row: K1, *p9, k1; rep from * to end.

Rep these 10 rows.

Large Eyelet Rib

Multiple of 6 + 2.

1st row (right side): *P2, k2tog, [yo] twice, sl 1, k1, psso; rep from * to last 2 sts, p2.

2nd row: K2, *p1, knit into first yo, purl into 2nd yo, p1, k2; rep from * to end.

3rd row: *P2, k4; rep from * to last 2 sts, p2.

4th row: K2, *p4, k2; rep from * to end.

Rep these 4 rows.

Double Basket Weave

Multiple of 4 + 3.

1st and every alt row (right side): Knit.

2nd row: *K3, p1; rep from * to last 3 sts, k3.

4th row: As 2nd row.

6th row: K1, *p1, k3; rep from * to last 2 sts, p1, k1.

8th row: As 6th row.

Rep these 8 rows.

Fleck Stitch

Multiple of 2 + 1.

1st row (right side): Knit.

2nd row: Purl.

3rd row: K1, *p1, k1; rep from * to end.

4th row: Purl.

Rep these 4 rows.

Sometimes just keeping it simple works best! Simple stitch, beautiful yarn and color!

Moss Stitch Diamonds

Multiple of 10 + 9.

1st row (right side): K4, *p1, k9; rep from * to last 5 sts, p1, k4.

2nd row: P3, *k1, p1, k1, p7; rep from * to last 6 sts, k1, p1, k1, p3.

3rd row: K2, *[p1, k1] twice, p1, k5; rep from * to last 7 sts, [p1, k1] twice, p1, k2.

4th row: [P1, k1] 4 times, *p3, [k1, p1] 3 times, k1; rep from * to last st, p1.

5th row: P1, *k1, p1; rep from * to end.

6th row: As 4th row.

7th row: As 3rd row.

8th row: As 2nd row.

9th row: As 1st row.

10th row: Purl.

Rep these 10 rows.

Horizontal Herringbone

Multiple of 2.

1st row (right side): K1, *sl 1, k1, psso but instead of dropping slipped st from left-hand needle, knit into the back of it; rep from * to last st, k1.

2nd row: *P2tog, then purl first st again slipping both sts off needle tog; rep from * to end.

Rep these 2 rows.

Check Stitch

Multiple of 4 + 2.

1st row: K2, *p2, k2; rep from * to end.

2nd row: P2, *k2, p2; rep from * to end.

Rep these last 2 rows once more.

5th row: As 2nd row.

6th row: As 1st row.

Rep these last 2 rows once more.

Rep these 8 rows.

Cactus Ladder

Multiple of 10 + 7.

1st row (right side): P3, KB1, *p4, KB1; rep from * to last 3 sts, p3.

2nd row: K3, PB1, *k4, PB1; rep from * to last 3 sts, k3.

3rd row: P2, [KB1] 3 times, *p3, KB1, p3, [KB1] 3 times; rep from * to last 2 sts, p2.

4th row: K2, [PB1] 3 times, *k3, PB1, k3, [PB1] 3 times; rep from * to last 2 sts, k2.

Rep the last 2 rows once more.

7th and 8th rows: As 1st and 2nd rows.

Rep the last 2 rows once more.

11th row: P3, KB1, p3, *[KB1] 3 times, p3, KB1, p3; rep from * to end.

12th row: K3, PB1, k3, *[PB1] 3 times, k3, PB1, k3; rep from * to end.

Rep the last 2 rows once more.

15th and 16th rows: As 1st and 2nd rows.

Rep these 16 rows.

Double Fleck Stitch

Multiple of 6 + 4.

1st and 3rd rows (right side): Knit.

2nd row: P4, *k2, p4; rep from * to end.

4th row: P1, *k2, p4; rep from * to last 3 sts, k2, p1.

Rep these 4 rows.

Most gauges for patterns are given for a 4in (10cm) square, but a 6in (15cm) square works best.

Moss Stitch Double Parallelograms

Multiple of 10.

1st row (right side): *K5, [p1, k1] twice, p1; rep from * to end.

2nd row: P1, *[k1, p1] twice, k1, p5; rep from * to last 9 sts, [k1, p1] twice, k1, p4.

3rd row: K3, *[p1, k1] twice, p1, k5; rep from * to last 7 sts, [p1, k1] twice, p1, k2.

4th row: P3, *[k1, p1] twice, k1, p5; rep from * to last 7 sts, [k1, p1] twice, k1, p2.

5th row: K1, *[p1, k1] twice, p1, k5; rep from * to last 9 sts, [p1, k1] twice, p1, k4.

6th row: *[P1, k1] twice, p5, k1; rep from * to end.

7th row: K1, p1, *k5, [p1, k1] twice, p1; rep from * to last 8 sts, k5, p1, k1, p1.

8th row: P1, k1, *p5, [k1, p1] twice, k1; rep from * to last 8 sts, p5, k1, p1, k1.

9th row: *[K1, p1] twice, k5, p1; rep from * to end.

10th row: *P5, [k1, p1] twice, k1; rep from * to end.

Rep these 10 rows.

Woven Rib

Multiple of 6 + 3.

1st row (right side): P3, *sl 1 purlwise, yb, k1, yf, sl 1 purlwise, p3; rep from * to end.

2nd row: K3, *p3, k3; rep from * to end.

3rd row: *P3, k1, yf, sl 1 purlwise, yb, k1; rep from * to last 3 sts, p3.

4th row: As 2nd row.

Rep these 4 rows.

Garter Stitch Checks

Multiple of 10 + 5.

1st row (right side): K5, *p5, k5; rep from * to end.

2nd row: Purl.

Rep the last 2 rows once more, then the 1st row again.

6th row: K5, *p5, k5; rep from * to end.

7th row: Knit.

Rep the last 2 rows once more, then the 6th row again.

Rep these 10 rows.

Flag Pattern 1

Multiple of 11.

1st row (right side): *P1, k10; rep from * to end.

2nd row: *P9, k2; rep from * to end.

3rd row: *P3, k8; rep from * to end.

4th row: *P7, k4; rep from * to end.

5th row: *P5, k6; rep from * to end.

6th row: As 5th row.

7th row: As 5th row.

8th row: As 4th row.

9th row: As 3rd row.

10th row: As 2nd row.

11th row: As 1st row.

12th row: *K1, p10; rep from * to end.

13th row: *K9, p2; rep from * to end.

14th row: *K3, p8; rep from * to end.

15th row: *K7, p4; rep from * to end.

16th row: *K5, p6; rep from * to end.

17th row: As 16th row.

18th row: As 16th row.

19th row: As 15th row.

20th row: As 14th row.

21st row: As 13th row.

22nd row: As 12th row.

Rep these 22 rows.

Crosses

Multiple of 12 + 1.

1st row (right side): Purl.

2nd row: Knit.

3rd row: P5, *[KB1] 3 times, p9; rep from * to last 8 sts, [KB1] 3 times, p5.

4th row: K5, *p3, k9; rep from * to last 8 sts, p3, k5.

Rep the last 2 rows once more.

7th row: P2, *[KB1] 9 times, p3; rep from * to last 11 sts, [KB1] 9 times, p2.

8th row: K2, *p9, k3; rep from * to last 11 sts, p9, k2.

Rep the last 2 rows once more.

11th row: As 3rd row.

12th row: As 4th row.

Rep the last 2 rows once more.

15th row: Purl.

16th row: Knit.

Rep these 16 rows.

Medallion Rib

Multiple of 8 + 4.

1st row (right side): P4, *yb, sl 2 purlwise, C2B, p4; rep from * to end.

2nd row: K4, *yf, sl 2 purlwise, purl the 2nd st on left-hand needle, then the 1st st, slipping both sts from needle tog, k4; rep from * to end.

3rd row: Knit.

4th row: Purl.

Rep these 4 rows.

Make a note of the gauge size on the handy pages at the back of this book, for future reference.

Reverse Stockinette Stitch Chevrons

Multiple of 6 + 5.

1st row (right side): K5, *p1, k5; rep from * to end.

2nd row: K1, *p3, k3; rep from * to last 4 sts, p3, k1.

3rd row: P2, *k1, p2; rep from * to end.

4th row: P1, *k3, p3; rep from * to last 4 sts, k3, p1.

5th row: K2, *p1, k5; rep from * to last 3 sts, p1, k2.

6th row: Purl.

Rep these 6 rows.

Stockinette Stitch Checks

Multiple of 10 + 5.

1st row (right side): K5, *p5, k5; rep from * to end.

2nd row: P5, *k5, p5; rep from * to end.

Rep the last 2 rows once more, then 1st row again.

6th row: K5, *p5, k5; rep from * to end.

7th row: As 2nd row.

Rep the last 2 rows once more, then 6th row again.

Rep these 10 rows.

Take just a little time to steam your swatch, pin it out and gently steam under a damp piece of cloth when you come to measure it will give a more accurate measurement.

Bordered Diamonds

Multiple of 16 + 2.

Note: Slip sts purlwise throughout.

1st row (right side): K6, *p6, k10; rep from * to last 12 sts, p6, k6.

2nd row: P5, sl 1, k6, yf, sl 1, *p8, sl 1, k6, yf, sl 1; rep from * to last 5 sts, p5.

3rd row: K5, *C2L, p4, C2R, k8; rep from * to last 13 sts, C2L, p4, C2R, k5.

4th row: P1, sl 1, p4, sl 1, k4, yf, sl 1, p1, *sl 2, p4, sl 1, k4, yf, sl 1, p4; rep from * to last 2 sts, sl 1, p1.

5th row: K1, *T2F, k3, C2L, p2, C2R, k3, T2B; rep from * to last st, k1.

6th row: P1, k1, yf, sl 1, p4, sl 1, *k2, yf, sl 1, p4, sl 1; rep from * to last 2 sts, k1, p1.

7th row: K1, p1, *T2F, k3, C2L, C2R, k3, T2B, p2; rep from * to last 16 sts, T2F, k3, C2L, C2R, k3, T2B, p1, k1.

8th row: P1, k2, yf, sl 1, *p4, sl 2, p4, sl 1, k4, yf, sl 1; rep from * to last 14 sts, p4, sl 2, p4, sl 1, k2, p1.

9th row: K1, p2, *T2F, k8, T2B, p4; rep from * to last 15 sts, T2F, k8, T2B, p2, k1.

10th row: P1, k3, yf, sl 1, *p8, sl 1, k6, yf, sl 1; rep from * to last 13 sts, p8, sl 1, k3, p1.

11th row: K1, p3, *k10, p6; rep from * to last 14 sts, k10, p3, k1.

12th row: As 10th row.

13th row: K1, p2, *C2R, k8 C2L, p4; rep from * to last 15 sts, C2R, k8, C2L, p2, k1.

14th row: As 8th row.

15th row: K1, p1, *C2R, k3, T2B, T2F, k3, C2L, p2; rep from * to last 16 sts, C2R, k3, T2B, T2F, k3, C2L, p1, k1.

16th row: As 6th row.

17th row: K1, *C2R, k3, T2B, p2, T2F, k3, C2L; rep from * to last st, k1.

18th row: As 4th row.

19th row: K5, *T2B, p4, T2F, k8; rep from * to last 13 sts, T2B, p4, T2F, k5.

20th row: As 2nd row.

Rep these 20 rows.

Ridged Rib

Multiple of 2 + 1.

1st and 2nd rows: Knit.

3rd row (right side): P1, *k1, p1; rep from * to end.

4th row: K1, *p1, k1; rep from * to end.

Rep these 4 rows.

Remember to note down the number of repeats, stitches and rows when creating a pattern so that you can remember these at a later point. Use the note pages in the back of this book.

Twisted Cable Rib

Multiple of 4 + 2.

1st row (right side): P2, *k2, p2; rep from * to end.

2nd row: K2, *p2, k2; rep from * to end.

3rd row: P2, *k2tog but do not slip off needle, then insert right-hand needle between these 2 sts and knit the 1st st again, slipping both sts off needle tog, p2; rep from * to end.

4th row: As 2nd row.

Rep these 4 rows.

Ladder Stitch

Multiple of 8 + 5.

1st row (right side): K5, *p3, k5; rep from * to end.

2nd row: P5, *k3, p5; rep from * to end.

Rep the last 2 rows once more.

5th row: K1, *p3, k5; rep from * to last 4 sts, p3, k1.

6th row: P1, *k3, p5; rep from * to last 4 sts, k3, p1.

Rep these last 2 rows once more.

Rep these 8 rows.

Small Basket Stitch

Multiple of 10 + 5.

1st row (right side): [K1, p1] twice, *k7, p1, k1, p1; rep from * to last st, k1.

2nd row: P1, [k1, p1] twice, *k5, [p1, k1] twice, p1; rep from * to end.

Rep the last 2 rows once more.

5th row: K6, *p1, k1, p1, k7; rep from * to last 9 sts, p1, k1, p1, k6.

6th row: *K5, [p1, k1] twice, p1; rep from * to last 5 sts, k5.

Rep the last 2 rows once more.

Rep these 8 rows.

Herringbone II

Multiple of 7 + 1.

Special Abbreviation: K1B Back = From the top, insert point of right-hand needle into back of st below next st on left-hand needle and knit it.

1st row (wrong side): Purl.

2nd row: *K2tog, k2, K1B Back then knit st above, k2; rep from * to last st, k1.

3rd row: Purl.

4th row: K3, K1B Back then knit st above, k2, k2tog, *k2, K1B Back then knit st above, k2, k2tog; rep from * to end. Rep these 4 rows.

When measuring use a steel ruler for best results, not a worn fabric tape which can often be stretched with constant use.

Double Moss Stitch
Triangles

Multiple of 8 + 1.

1st row (right side): *K1, p7; rep from * to last st, k1.

2nd row: *P1, k7; rep from * to last st, p1.

3rd row: *P1, k1, p5, k1; rep from * to last st, p1.

4th row: *K1, p1, k5, p1; rep from * to last st, k1.

5th row: K1, p1, *k1, p3, [k1, p1] twice; rep from * to last 7 sts, k1, p3, k1, p1, k1.

6th row: P1, k1, *p1, k3, [p1, k1] twice; rep from * to last 7 sts, p1, k3, p1, k1, p1.

7th row: *P1, k1; rep from * to last st, p1.

8th row: *K1, p1; rep from * to last st, k1.

9th row: P4, *k1, p7; rep from * to last 5 sts, k1, p4.

10th row: K4, *p1, k7; rep from * to last 5 sts, p1, k4.

11th row: P3, *k1, p1, k1, p5; rep from * to last 6 sts, k1, p1, k1, p3.

12th row: K3, *p1, k1, p1, k5; rep from * to last 6 sts, p1, k1, p1, k3.

13th row: P2, *[k1, p1] twice, k1, p3; rep from * to last 7 sts, [k1, p1] twice, k1, p2.

14th row: K2, *[p1, k1] twice, p1, k3; rep from * to last 7 sts, [p1, k1] twice, p1, k2.

15th row: As 7th row.

16th row: As 8th row.

Rep these 16 rows.

Spaced Knots

Multiple of 6 + 5.

Note: Stitches should not be counted after the 5th or 11th rows.

Work 4 rows in st st, starting knit.

5th row: K5, *[k1, p1] twice into next st, k5; rep from * to end.

6th row: P5, *sl 3, k1, pass 3 sl sts separately over last st (knot completed), p5; rep from * to end.

Work 4 rows in st st.

11th row: K2, *[k1, p1] twice into next st, k5; rep from * to last 3 sts, [k1, p1] twice into next st, k2.

12th row: P2, *sl 3, k1, pass sl sts over as before, p5; rep from * to last 6 sts, sl 3, k1, pass sl sts over as before, p2.

Rep these 12 rows.

Uneven Rib

Multiple of 4 + 3.

1st row: *K2, p2; rep from * to last 3 sts, k2, p1.

Rep this row.

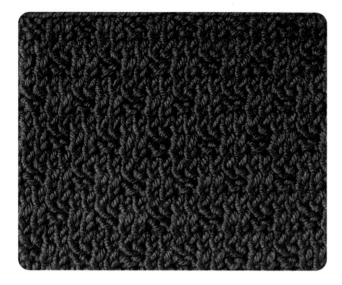

Twisted Check

Multiple of 4 + 2.

1st row (right side): Knit all sts through back loops.

2nd row: Purl.

3rd row: [KB1] twice, *p2, [KB1] twice; rep from * to end.

4th row: P2, *k2, p2; rep from * to end.

Rep 1st and 2nd rows once more.

7th row: P2, *[KB1] twice, p2; rep from * to end.

8th row: K2, *p2, k2; rep from * to end.

Rep these 8 rows.

Topiary Stitch

Multiple of 24 + 3.

1st row (right side): P1, KB1, *p5, KB1, [p1, KB1] 6 times, p5, KB1; rep from * to last st, p1.

2nd row: K1, p1, *k5, p1, [k1, p1] 6 times, k5, p1; rep from * to last st, k1.

3rd row: As 1st row.

4th row: K1, p1, *k7, p1, [k1, p1] 4 times, k7, p1; rep from * to last st, k1.

5th row: P1, KB1, *p7, KB1, [p1, KB1] 4 times, p7, KB1; rep from * to last st, p1.

6th row: K1, p1, k9, p1, [k1, p1] twice, *[k9, p1] twice, [k1, p1] twice; rep from * to last 11 sts, k9, p1, k1.

7th row: P1, KB1, p9, KB1, [p1, KB1] twice, *[p9, KB1]

twice, [p1, KB1] twice; rep from * to last 11 sts, p9, KB1, p1.

8th row: K1, p1, *k11, p1; rep from * to last st, k1.

9th row: P1, KB1, *p11, KB1; rep from * to last st, p1.

10th row: *[K1, p1] twice, [k9, p1] twice; rep from * to last 3 sts, k1, p1, k1.

11th row: *[P1, KB1] twice, [p9, KB1] twice; rep from * to last 3 sts, p1, KB1, p1.

12th row: [K1, p1] 3 times, [k7, p1] twice, *[k1, p1] 4 times, [k7, p1] twice; rep from * to last 5 sts, k1, [p1, k1] twice.

13th row: [P1, KB1] 3 times, [p7, KB1] twice, *[p1, KB1] 4 times, [p7, KB1] twice; rep from * to last 5 sts, p1, [KB1, p1] twice.

14th row: [K1, p1] 4 times, [k5, p1] twice, *[k1, p1] 6 times, [k5, p1] twice; rep from * to last 7 sts, k1, [p1, k1] 3 times.

15th row: [P1, KB1] 4 times, [p5, KB1] twice, *[p1, KB1] 6 times, [p5, KB1] twice; rep from * to last 7 sts, p1, [KB1, p1] 3 times.

Rep the last 2 rows twice more.

20th and 21st rows: As 12th and 13th rows.

22nd and 23rd rows: As 10th and 11th rows.

24th and 25th rows: As 8th and 9th rows.

26th and 27th rows: As 6th and 7th rows.

28th and 29th rows: As 4th and 5th rows.

30th row: As 2nd row.

31st and 32nd rows: As 1st and 2nd rows.

Rep these 32 rows.

Dotted Ladder Stitch

Multiple of 8 + 5.

1st row (right side): K2, p1, k2, *p3, k2, p1, k2; rep from * to end.

2nd row: [P1, k1] twice, p1, *k3, [p1, k1] twice, p1; rep from * to end.

Rep the last 2 rows once more.

5th row: K1, *p3, k2, p1, k2; rep from * to last 4 sts, p3, k1.

6th row: P1, k3, p1, *[k1, p1] twice, k3, p1; rep from * to end.

Rep these last 2 rows once more.

Rep these 8 rows.

Knot Pattern

Multiple of 6 + 5.

Special Abbreviation: Make knot = p3 tog leaving sts on left-hand needle, now knit them tog, then purl then tog again, slipping sts off needle at end.

Work 2 rows in st st, starting knit.

3rd row (right side): K1, *make knot (see Special Abbreviation), k3; rep from * to last 4 sts, make knot, k1.

Work 3 rows in st st, starting purl.

7th row: K4, *make knot, k3; rep from * to last st, k1.

8th row: Purl.

Rep these 8 rows.

Always measure on a flat surface like a tabletop—never on your lap, arm of armchair or carpet.

Trellis Stitch 1

Multiple of 6 + 5.

1st row (right side): K1, p3, *keeping yarn at front of work sl 3 purlwise, p3; rep from * to last st, k1.

2nd row: P1, k3, *keeping yarn at back of work sl 3 purlwise, k3; rep from * to last st, p1.

3rd row: K1, p3, *k3, p3; rep from * to last st, k1.

4th row: P1, k3, *p3, k3; rep from * to last st, p1.

5th row: K5, *insert point of right-hand needle upwards under the 2 strands in front of the sl sts and knit the next st, then lift the 2 strands off over the point of the right-hand needle (called pull up loop), k5; rep from * to end.

6th row: As 3rd row.

7th row: P1, *keeping yarn at front sl 3 purlwise, p3; rep from * to last 4 sts, sl 3 purlwise, p1.

8th row: K1, *keeping yarn at back sl 3 purlwise, k3; rep from * to last 4 sts, sl 3 purlwise, k1.

9th row: As 4th row.

10th row: As 3rd row.

11th row: K2, *pull up loop, k5; rep from * to last 3 sts, pull up loop, k2.

12th row: As 4th row.

Rep these 12 rows.

Puffed Rib

Multiple of 3 + 2.

Note: Stitches should only be counted after the 4th row.

1st row (right side): P2, *yon, k1, yfrn, p2; rep from * to end.

2nd row: K2, *p3, k2; rep from * to end.

3rd row: P2, *k3, p2; rep from * to end.

4th row: K2, *p3tog, k2; rep from * to end.

Rep these 4 rows.

Think about using the swatches you make into a project themselves—a patchwork cushion, baby blanket, scented sachets, even a frame for a small picture.

Interrupted Rib

Multiple of 2 + 1.

1st row (right side): P1, *k1, p1; rep from * to end.

2nd row: K1, *p1, k1; rep from * to end.

3rd row: Purl.

4th row: Knit.

Rep these 4 rows.

When designing for the home, think about what the project may sit with—contrast and complimentary textures such as wood, metal, glass, stone, or fabric.

Bud Stitch

Multiple of 6 + 5.

Note: Stitches should only be counted after the 6th or 12th rows.

1st row (right side): P5, *k1, yfrn, p5; rep from * to end.

2nd row: K5, *p2, k5; rep from * to end.

3rd row: P5, *k2, p5; rep from * to end.

Rep the last 2 rows once more.

6th row: K5, *p2tog, k5; rep from * to end.

7th row: P2, *k1, yfrn, p5; rep from * to last 3 sts, k1, yfrn, p2.

8th row: K2, *p2, k5; rep from * to last 4 sts, p2, k2.

9th row: P2, *k2, p5; rep from * to last 4 sts, k2, p2.

Rep the last 2 rows once more.

12th row: K2, *p2tog, k5; rep from * to last 4 sts, p2tog, k2.

Rep these 12 rows.

Garter Slip Stitch V

Multiple of 2 + 1.

1st row (right side): Knit.

2nd row: Knit.

3rd row: K1, *sl 1 purlwise, k1; rep from * to end.

4th row: K1, *yf, sl 1 purlwise, yb, k1; rep from * to end.

Knit 2 rows.

7th row: K2, *sl 1 purlwise, k1; rep from * to last st, k1.

8th row: K2, *yf, sl 1 purlwise, yb, k1; rep from * to last st, k1.

Rep these 8 rows.

If you are designing a garment, take your swatches and pin them onto an old sweater or shape that you like to get a sense of scale and what it might look like. Alternatively, pin the swatch onto a stand or dress form if you have access to one (a patient family member will do as well) and work out the stitches and rows required.

Compass Check Pattern

Multiple of 14 + 7.

1st row (wrong side): [P1, KB1] twice, *k10, [p1, KB1] twice; rep from * to last 3 sts, k3.

2nd row: K3, [PB1, k1] twice, *p7, k3, [PB1, k1] twice; rep from * to end.

Rep the last 2 rows once more.

5th row: Knit.

6th row: [K1, PB1] twice, *p10, [k1, PB1] twice; rep from * to last 3 sts, p3.

7th row: P3, [KB1, p1] twice, *k7, p3, [KB1, p1] twice; rep from * to end.

Rep the last 2 rows once more.

10th row: P7, *[k1, PB1] twice, p10; rep from * to end.

11th row: K7, *p3, [KB1, p1] twice, k7; rep from * to end.

Rep the last 2 rows once more.

14th row: Purl.

15th row: K7, *[p1, KB1] twice, k10; rep from * to end.

16th row: P7, *k3, [PB1, k1] twice, p7; rep from * to end.

Rep the last 2 rows once more.

Rep these 18 rows.

Mock Cable on Moss Stitch

Multiple of 9 + 5.

1st row (right side): [K1, p1] twice, k1, *KB1, p2, KB1, [k1, p1] twice, k1; rep from * to end.

2nd row: *[K1, p1] 3 times, k2, p1; rep from * to last 5 sts, [k1, p1] twice, k1.

Rep these 2 rows once more.

5th row: [K1, p1] twice, k1, *yo, k1, p2, k1, lift yo over last 4 sts and off needle, [k1, p1] twice, k1; rep from * to end.

6th row: As 2nd row.

Rep these 6 rows.

Steps

Multiple of 8 + 2.

1st row (right side): *K4, p4; rep from * to last 2 sts, k2.

2nd row: P2, *k4, p4; rep from * to end.

Rep the last 2 rows once more.

5th row: K2, *p4, k4; rep from * to end.

6th row: *P4, k4; rep from * to last 2 sts, p2.

7th row: As 5th row.

8th row: As 6th row.

9th row: *P4, k4; rep from * to last 2 sts, p2.

10th row: K2, *p4, k4; rep from * to end.

Rep the last 2 rows once more.

13th row: As 2nd row.

14th row: *K4, p4; rep from * to last 2 sts, k2.

Rep the last 2 rows once more.

Rep these 16 rows.

When creating a garment design, think about assembling the swatches onto a mood board. Consider adding the trims, buttons, ribbons edging you may wish to use. I often add buttons to the swatch for future reference to make sure they work with the design and don't get lost!

Bramble Stitch 1

Multiple of 4 + 2.

1st row (right side): Purl.

2nd row: K1, *(k1, p1, k1) into next st, p3tog; rep from * to last st, k1.

3rd row: Purl.

4th row: K1, *p3tog, (k1, p1, k1) into next st; rep from * to last st, k1.

Rep these 4 rows.

Lattice Stitch

Multiple of 6 + 1.

1st row (right side): K3, *p1, k5; rep from * to last 4 sts, p1, k3.

2nd row: P2, *k1, p1, k1, p3; rep from * to last 5 sts, k1, p1, k1, p2.

3rd row: K1, *p1, k3, p1, k1; rep from * to end.

4th row: K1, *p5, k1; rep from * to end.

5th row: As 3rd row.

6th row: As 2nd row.

Rep these 6 rows.

Slanting Diamonds

Multiple of 10.

1st row (right side): *K9, p1; rep from * to end.

2nd row: *K2, p8; rep from * to end.

3rd row: *K7, p3; rep from * to end.

4th row: *K4, p6; rep from * to end.

5th and 6th rows: *K5, p5; rep from * to end.

7th row: K5, p4, *k6, p4; rep from * to last st, k1.

8th row: P2, k3, *p7, k3; rep from * to last 5 sts, p5.

9th row: K5, p2, *k8, p2; rep from * to last 3 sts, k3.

10th row: P4, k1, *p9, k1; rep from * to last 5 sts, p5.

11th row: K4, p1, *k9, p1; rep from * to last 5 sts, k5.

12th row: P5, k2, *p8, k2; rep from * to last 3 sts, p3.

13th row: K2, p3, *k7, p3; rep from * to last 5 sts, k5.

14th row: P5, k4, *p6, k4; rep from * to last st, p1.

15th and 16th rows: *P5, k5; rep from * to end.

17th row: *P4, k6; rep from * to end.

18th row: *P7, k3; rep from * to end.

19th row: *P2, k8; rep from * to end.

20th row: *P9, k1; rep from * to end.

Rep these 20 rows.

Diagonal Bobble Stitch

Multiple of 6.

1st row (right side): *K2, Make Bobble (MB) as follows: [knit into front and back] 3 times into next st, take 1st, 2nd, 3rd, 4th and 5th sts over 6th made st, (bobble completed), p3; rep from * to end.

2nd row: *K3, p3; rep from * to end.

3rd row: P1, *k2, MB, p3; rep from * to last 5 sts, k2, MB, p2.

4th row: K2, *p3, k3; rep from * to last 4 sts, p3, k1.

5th row: P2, *k2, MB, p3; rep from * to last 4 sts, k2, MB, p1.

6th row: K1, *p3, k3; rep from * to last 5 sts, p3, k2.

7th row: *P3, k2, MB: rep from * to end.

8th row: *P3, k3; rep from * to end.

9th row: *MB, p3, k2; rep from * to end.

10th row: P2, *k3, p3; rep from * to last 4 sts, k3, p1.

11th row: K1, *MB, p3, k2; rep from * to last 5 sts, MB, p3, k1.

12th row: P1, *k3, p3; rep from * to last 5 sts, k3, p2.

Rep these 12 rows.

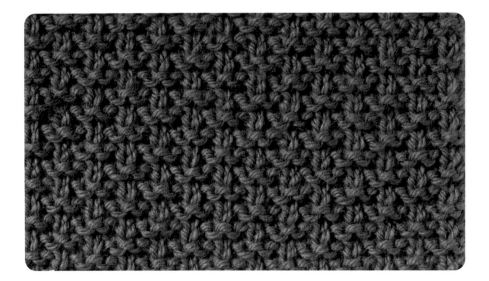

Basket Weave

Multiple of 4 + 3.

1st and 3rd rows (right side): Knit.

2nd row: *K3, p1; rep from * to last 3 sts, k3.

4th row: K1, *p1, k3; rep from * to last 2 sts, p1, k1.

Rep these 4 rows.

Make sure your swatch and fabric are fit for the purpose of your project.

Mini Bobble Stitch 1

Multiple of 2 + 1.

Special Abbreviation: MB (Make Bobble) = work (p1, k1, p1, k1) all into next st, pass 2nd, 3rd and 4th sts over first st.

1st row (right side): Knit.

2nd row: K1, *MB (see Special Abbreviation), k1; rep from * to end.

3rd row: Knit.

4th row: K2, *MB, k1; rep from * to last st, k1.

Rep these 4 rows.

Basket Rib 1

Multiple of 2 + 1.

1st row (right side): Knit.

2nd row: Purl.

3rd row: K1, *sl 1 purlwise, k1; rep from * to end.

4th row: K1, *yf, sl 1 purlwise, yb, k1; rep from * to end.

Rep these 4 rows.

Shingle Stitch

Multiple of 10 + 5.

1st row (right side): K5, *KB1, [p1, KB1] twice, k5; rep from * to end.

2nd row: K5, *PB1, [k1, PB1] twice, k5; rep from * to end.

Rep the last 2 rows twice more.

7th row: KB1, [p1, KB1] twice, *k5, KB1, [p1, KB1] twice; rep from * to end.

8th row: PB1, [k1, PB1] twice, *k5, PB1, [k1, PB1] twice; rep from * to end.

Rep the last 2 rows twice more.

Rep these 12 rows.

Twisted Stockinette Stitch

Any number of stitches.

1st row (right side): Knit into the back of every st.

2nd row: Purl.

Rep these 2 rows.

If you knit (plain) the first right-side row when you change colors, you will get a clean-cut change of stripe also in reverse stockinette stitch. Play around with the many possibilities within one garment. The result will be fascinating patterns which gives knitting stripes a whole new aspect.

Harbor Flag

Multiple of 10.

1st row (right side): P7, k2, *p8, k2; rep from * to last st, p1.

2nd row: *P1, k1, p2, k6; rep from * to end.

3rd row: *P5, k2, p1, k2; rep from * to end.

4th row: *P3, k1, p2, k4; rep from * to end.

5th row: *P3, k2, p1, k4; rep from * to end.

6th row: *P5, k1, p2, k2; rep from * to end.

7th row: *P1, k2, p1, k6; rep from * to end.

8th row: As 6th row.

9th row: As 5th row.

10th row: As 4th row.

11th row: As 3rd row.

12th row: As 2nd row.

13th row: As 1st row.

14th row: *P2, k8; rep from * to end.

Rep these 14 rows.

Alternating Triangles

Multiple of 5.

1st row (right side): *P1, k4; rep from * to end.

2nd and 3rd rows: *P3, k2; rep from * to end.

4th row: *P1, k4; rep from * to end.

5th row: *K4, p1; rep from * to end.

6th and 7th rows: *K2, p3; rep from * to end.

8th row: As 5th row.

Rep these 8 rows.

Ridge and Furrow

Worked over 23 sts on a background of st st.

1st row (right side): P4, k7, p1, k7, p4.

2nd row: K1, p2, k1, p5, [k1, p1] twice, k1, p5, k1, p2, k1.

3rd row: P4, k4, [p1, k2] twice, p1, k4, p4.

4th row: K1, p2, [k1, p3] 4 times, k1, p2, k1.

5th row: P4, k2, [p1, k4] twice, p1, k2, p4.

6th row: K1, p2, k1, p1, [k1, p5] twice, k1, p1, k1, p2, k1.

Rep these 6 rows.

To prevent loose spots where two ends meet when knitting on the round, cast on one extra stitch. When joining to a circle, knit the first and last stitch together.

Half Brioche Stitch (Purl Version)

Multiple of 2 + 1.

1st row (wrong side): Purl.

2nd row: K1, *K1B, k1; rep from * to end.

3rd row: Purl.

4th row: K1B, *k1, K1B; rep from * to end.

Rep these 4 rows.

Moss Slip Stitch 1

Multiple of 2 + 1.

1st row (right side): K1, *sl 1 purlwise, k1; rep from * to end.

2nd row: K1, *yf, sl 1 purlwise, yb, k1; rep from * to end.

3rd row: K2, *sl 1 purlwise, k1; rep from * to last st, k1.

4th row: K2, *yf, sl 1 purlwise, yb, k1; rep from * to last st, k1.

Rep these 4 rows.

Biba Trellis

Multiple of 14 + 5.

Note: Slip sts purlwise with yarn at wrong side of work.

1st row (right side): Purl.

2nd row: Knit.

3rd row: Purl.

4th row: P8, sl 3, *p11, sl 3; rep from * to last 8 sts, p8.

5th row: K8, sl 3, *k11, sl 3; rep from * to last 8 sts, k8.

Rep the last 2 rows once more, then 4th row again.

9th, 10th and 11th rows: As 1st, 2nd and 3rd rows.

12th row: P1, sl 3, *p11, sl 3; rep from * to last st, p1.

13th row: K1, sl 3, *k11, sl 3; rep from * to last st, k1.

Rep the last 2 rows once more, then 12th row again.

Rep these 16 rows.

Diagonal Checks

Multiple of 5 sts.

1st row (right side): *P1, k4; rep from * to end.

2nd row: *P3, k2; rep from * to end.

3rd row: As 2nd row.

4th row: *P1, k4; rep from * to end.

5th row: *K1, p4; rep from * to end.

6th row: *K3, p2; rep from * to end.

7th row: As 6th row.

8th row: As 5th row.

Rep these 8 rows.

Slipped Rib 1

Multiple of 4 + 3.

1st row (right side): K1, sl 1 purlwise, *k3, sl 1 purlwise; rep from * to last st, k1.

2nd row: P1, sl 1 purlwise, *p3, sl 1 purlwise; rep from * to last st, p1.

3rd row: *K3, sl 1 purlwise; rep from * to last 3 sts, k3.

4th row: *P3, sl 1 purlwise; rep from * to last 3 sts, p3.

Rep these 4 rows.

Diagonal Rib

Multiple of 4.

1st row (right side): *K2, p2; rep from * to end.

2nd row: As 1st row.

3rd row: K1, *p2, k2; rep from * to last 3 sts, p2, k1.

4th row: P1, *k2, p2; rep from * to last 3 sts, k2, p1.

5th row: *P2, k2; rep from * to end.

6th row: As 5th row.

7th row: As 4th row.

8th row: As 3rd row

Rep these 8 rows.

Pop can rings make great cost-effective markers for knitting!

Garter Stitch Twisted Rib

Multiple of 4.

1st row (right side): K1, *C2B, k2; rep from * to last 3 sts, C2B, k1.

2nd row: K1, *yf, C2P, yb, k2; rep from * to last 3 sts, yf, C2P, yb, k1.

Rep these 2 rows.

Use markers to denote the beginning and end of pattern repeats or every 20–25 stitches for a project that requires a lot of counting.

Tree of Life

Worked over 23 sts on a background of st st.

1st row (right side): P4, k7, p1, k7, p4.

2nd row: K1, p2, k1, p6, k1, p1, k1, p6, k1, p2, k1.

3rd row: P4, k5, p1, k3, p1, k5, p4.

4th row: K1, p2, k1, p4, [k1, p2] twice, k1, p4, k1, p2, k1.

5th row: P4, k3, p1, k2, p1, k1, p1, k2, p1, k3, p4.

6th row: [K1, p2] 3 times, k1, p3, [k1, p2] 3 times, k1.

7th row: P4, k1, [p1, k2] 4 times, p1, k1, p4.

8th row: K1, p2, k1, p3, k1, p2, k1, p1, k1, p2, k1, p3, k1, p2, k1.

9th row: P4, [k2, p1] twice, k3, [p1, k2] twice, p1.

10th row: As 4th row.

11th row: As 5th row.

12th row: K1, p2, k1, p5, k1, p3, k1, p5, k1, p2, k1.

13th row: P4, k4, [p1, k2] twice, p1, k4, p4.

14th row: As 2nd row.

15th row: As 3rd row.

16th row: K1, p2, k1, [p7, k1] twice, p2, k1.

17th row: P4, k6, p1, k1, p1, k6, p4.

18th row: K1, p2, k1, p15, k1, p2, k1.

19th row: As 1st row.

20th row: As 18th row.

Rep these 20 rows.

Moss Panels

Multiple of 8 + 7.

1st row (wrong side): K3, *p1, k3; rep from * to end.

2nd row: P3, *k1, p3; rep from * to end.

3rd row: K2, p1, k1, *[p1, k2] twice, p1, k1; rep from * to last 3 sts, p1, k2.

4th row: P2, k1, p1, *[k1, p2] twice, k1, p1; rep from * to last 3 sts, k1, p2.

5th row: K1, *p1, k1; rep from * to end.

6th row: P1, *k1, p1; rep from * to end.

7th row: As 3rd row.

8th row: As 4th row.

9th row: As 1st row.

10th row: As 2nd row.

Rep these 10 rows.

Garter Stitch Steps

Multiple of 8.

1st and every alt row (right side): Knit.

2nd and 4th rows: *K4, p4; rep from * to end.

6th and 8th rows: K2, *p4, k4; rep from * to last 6 sts, p4, k2.

10th and 12th rows: *P4, k4; rep from * to end.

14th and 16th rows: P2, *k4, p4; rep from * to last 6 sts, k4, p2.

Rep these 16 rows.

When sewing shoulders together, use sock needles—they hold everything in place without damaging the garment.

Knotted Rib

Multiple of 5.

Note: Stitches should only be counted after the 2nd row.

1st row (right side): P2, *knit into front and back of next st, p4; rep from * to last 3 sts, knit into front and back of next st, p2.

2nd row: K2, *p2tog, k4; rep from * to last 4 sts, p2tog, k2.

Rep these 2 rows.

Lightly spraying starch on embroidery, cables and other types of textured knitting while they're blocking will set them nicely.

3-Stitch Twisted Rib

Multiple of 5 + 2.

1st row (wrong side): K2, *p3, k2; rep from * to end.

2nd row: P2, *C3, p2; rep from * to end.

Rep these 2 rows.

Triple Wave

Worked over 14 sts on a background of st st.

1st row (right side): P3, k8, p3.

2nd row: [K1, p1] twice, k2, p2, k2, [p1, k1] twice.

3rd row: P3, k3, p2, k3, p3.

4th row: K1, p1, k1, p8, k1, p1, k1.

5th row: P3, k1, p2, k2, p2, k1, p3.

6th row: K1, p1, k1, p3, k2, p3, k1, p1, k1.

Rep these 6 rows.

When you are starting a sweater on circular needles, knit the ribbing back one row before you join the ends and start circular knitting to keep the cast-on row from twisting on you.

Linked Ribs

Multiple of 8 + 4.

1st row (right side): P4, *k1, p2, k1, p4; rep from * to end.

2nd row: K4, *p1, k2, p1, k4; rep from * to end.

Rep the last 2 rows once more.

5th row: P4, *C2L, C2R, p4; rep from * to end.

6th row: K4, *p4, k4; rep from * to end.

Rep these 6 rows.

Purled Ladder Stitch

Multiple of 4 + 2.

1st and 2nd rows: Knit.

3rd row (right side): P2, *k2, p2; rep from * to end.

4th row: K2, *p2, k2; rep from * to end.

5th and 6th rows: Knit.

7th row: As 4th row.

8th row: P2, *k2, p2; rep from * to end.

Rep these 8 rows.

Broken Rib

Multiple of 2 + 1.

1st row (right side): Knit.

2nd row: P1, *k1, p1; rep from * to end.

Rep these 2 rows.

Sometimes, if you slip the first stitch, it will give a nice smooth edge to the finished piece.

Rose Stitch

Multiple of 2 + 1.

1st row (wrong side): K2, *p1, k1; rep from * to last st, k1.

2nd row: K1, *K1B, k1; rep from * to end.

3rd row: K1, *p1, k1; rep from * to end.

4th row: K2, *K1B, k1; rep from * to last st, k1.

Rep these 4 rows.

You've heard it countless times before, but always do a swatch before starting a project no matter how skilled of a knitter you are.

Moss Rib

Multiple of 4 + 1.

1st row: K2, *p1, k3; rep from * to last 3 sts, p1, k2.

2nd row: P1, *k3, p1; rep from * to end.

Rep these 2 rows.

Embossed Rib

Multiple of 6 + 2.

1st row (right side): P2, *KB1, k1, p1, KB1, p2; rep from * to end.

2nd row: K2, *PB1, k1, p1, PB1, k2; rep from * to end.

3rd row: P2, *KB1, p1, k1, KB1, p2; rep from * to end.

4th row: K2, *PB1, p1, k1, PB1, k2; rep from * to end.

Rep these 4 rows.

Use a pair of needles that is one size larger to cast on so that the cast-on row isn't tight when knitting the first row.

Anchor

Worked over 17 sts on a background of st st.

1st row (right side): P3, k11, p3.

2nd row: K1, p1, [k1, p5] twice, k1, p1, k1.

3rd row: P3, k4, p1, k1, p1, k4, p3.

4th row: K1, p1, k1, p3, [k1, p1] twice, k1, p3, k1, p1, k1.

5th row: P3, k2, p1, k5, p1, k2, p3.

6th row: [K1, p1] twice, [k1, p3] twice, [k1, p1] twice, k1.

7th row: P3, k1, p1, k7, p1, k1, p3.

8th row: K1, p1, [k1, p5] twice, k1, p1, k1.

9th row: As 1st row.

Rep the last 2 rows once more.

12th row: K1, p1, k1, p3, k5, p3, k1, p1, k1.

13th row: P3, k3, p5, k3, p3.

14th row: As 12th row.

15th row: As 1st row.

16th row: As 8th row.

Rep the last 2 rows once more.

19th row: As 3rd row.

20th row: K1, p1, [k1, p3] 3 times, k1, p1, k1.

21st row: As 3rd row.

22nd row: As 2nd row.

23rd row: As 1st row.

24th row: K1, p1, k1, p11, k1, p1, k1.

Rep these 24 rows.

Chevron Rib 1

Multiple of 18 + 1.

1st row (right side): P1, *k1, p2, k2, p2, k1, p1; rep from * to end.

2nd row: *K3, p2, k2, p2, k1, [p2, k2] twice; rep from * to last st, k1.

3rd row: *[P2, k2] twice, p3, k2, p2, k2, p1; rep from * to last st, p1.

4th row: *K1, p2, k2, p2, k5, p2, k2, p2; rep from * to last st, k1.

Rep these 4 rows.

Remember to take a break every 45 minutes or so, this will prevent tired wrists and help to keep you focused when you return to the pattern.

Tile Stitch

Multiple of 6 + 4.

1st row (right side): K4, *p2, k4; rep from * to end.

2nd row: P4, *k2, p4; rep from * to end.

Rep the last 2 rows twice more.

7th row: As 2nd row.

8th row: K4, *p2, k4; rep from * to end.

Rep these 8 rows.

Twisted Moss 1

Multiple of 2 + 1.

1st row (wrong side): Knit.

2nd row: K1, *K1B, k1; rep from * to end.

3rd row: Knit.

4th row: K1B, *k1, K1B; rep from * to end.

Rep these 4 rows.

Divided Boxes

Multiple of 5.

1st row (right side): Knit.

2nd row: *K1, p4; rep from * to end.

3rd row: *K3, p2; rep from * to end.

4th row: As 3rd row.

5th row: As 2nd row.

6th row: Knit.

Rep these 6 rows.

When knitting socks, use the tail to mark the beginning of the round.

Diamond Net Mask

Worked over 19 sts on a background of st st.

1st row (right side): P3, k6, p1, k6, p3.

2nd row: K1, p1, k1, [p6, k1] twice, p1, k1.

3rd row: P3, k5, p1, k1, p1, k5, p3.

4th row: K1, p1, k1, [p5, k1, p1, k1] twice.

5th row: P3, k4, [p1, k1] twice, p1, k4, p3.

6th row: K1, p1, k1, p4, [k1, p1] twice, k1, p4, k1, p1, k1.

7th row: P3, k3, [p1, k1] 3 times, p1, k3, p3.

8th row: K1, p1, k1, p3, [k1, p1] 3 times, k1, p3, k1, p1, k1.

9th row: P3, k2, p1, k1, p1, k3, p1, k1, p1, k2, p3.

10th row: K1, p1, k1, p2, k1, p1, k1, p3, k1, p1, k1, p2, k1, p1, k1.

11th row: P3, [k1, p1] twice, k5, [p1, k1] twice, p3.

12th row: [K1, p1] 3 times, k1, p5, [k1, p1] 3 times, k1.

13th row: As 9th row.

14th row: As 10th row.

15th row: As 7th row.

16th row: As 8th row.

17th row: As 5th row.

18th row: As 6th row.

19th row: As 3rd row.

20th row: As 4th row.

Rep these 20 rows.

Moss Diamonds

Multiple of 10 + 7.

1st row (right side): *[K3, p1] twice, k1, p1; rep from * to last 7 sts, k3, p1, k3.

2nd row: *[P3, k1] twice, p1, k1; rep from * to last 7 sts, p3, k1, p3.

3rd row: K2, p1, k1, p1, *[k3, p1] twice, k1, p1; rep from * to last 2 sts, k2.

4th row: P2, k1, p1, k1, *[p3, k1] twice, p1, k1; rep from * to last 2 sts, p2.

5th row: [K1, p1] 3 times, *[k2, p1] twice, [k1, p1] twice; rep from * to last st, k1.

6th row: [P1, k1] 3 times, *[p2, k1] twice, [p1, k1] twice; rep from * to last st, p1.

7th row: As 3rd row.

8th row: As 4th row.

9th row: As 1st row.

10th row: As 2nd row.

11th row: K3, p1, *k2, [p1, k1] twice, p1, k2, p1; rep from * to last 3 sts, k3.

12th row: P3, k1, *p2, [k1, p1] twice, k1, p2, k1; rep from * to last 3 sts, p3.

Rep these 12 rows.

Woven Stitch

Multiple of 4 + 2.

1st row (right side): Knit.

2nd row: Purl.

3rd row: K2, *p2, k2; rep from * to end.

4th row: P2, *k2, p2; rep from * to end.

5th row: Knit.

6th row: Purl.

7th row: As 4th row.

8th row: As 3rd row.

Rep these 8 rows.

Large needles and chunky yarn are popular for quick-fix projects. If you're short on time, scarves on size 17 needles can be knitted in a matter of moments.

Stockinette Stitch Ridge 1

Multiple of 2.

Note: Stitches should not be counted after the 2nd row.

1st row (right side): Knit.

2nd row: P1, *k2tog; rep from * to last st, p1.

3rd row: K1, *knit into front and back of next st; rep from * to last st, k1.

4th row: Purl.

Rep these 4 rows.

Centipede Stitch

Multiple of 6 + 4.

1st row (right side): Knit.

2nd row: P1, k2, *p4, k2; rep from * to last st, p1.

Rep the last 2 rows 5 times more.

13th row: Knit.

14th row: P4, *k2, p4; rep from * to end.

Rep the last 2 rows 5 times more.

Rep these 24 rows.

Caterpillar Stitch

Multiple of 8 + 6.

1st row (right side): K4, p2, *k6, p2; rep from * to end.

2nd row: P1, k2, *p6, k2; rep from * to last 3 sts, p3.

3rd row: K2, p2, *k6, p2; rep from * to last 2 sts, k2.

4th row: P3, k2, *p6, k2; rep from * to last st, p1.

5th row: P2, *k6, p2; rep from * to last 4 sts, k4.

6th row: Purl.

Rep these 6 rows.

Almost all knitting patterns have you cast on and begin the first row as the right side which makes the back part of your cast-on stitch on the visible side.

Little Chevron Rib

Multiple of 10 + 1.

1st row (right side): P1, *k1, p1, [k2, p1] twice, k1, p1; rep from * to end.

2nd row: K1, *p2, [k1, p1] twice, k1, p2, k1; rep from * to end.

3rd row: P1, *k3, p3, k3, p1; rep from * to end.

4th row: K2, *p3, k1, p3, k3; rep from * to last 9 sts, p3, k1, p3, k2.

Rep these 4 rows.

When working with slinky yarns, wind them up into center-pull balls and insert them into the leg of an old pair of stockings to prevent tangling.

Open Twisted Rib

Multiple of 5 + 3.

Note: Sts should not be counted after the 2nd or 3rd rows of this pattern.

1st row (wrong side): K1, PB1, k1, *p2, k1, PB1, k1; rep from * to end.

2nd row: P1, KB1, p1, *k1, yo, k1, p1, KB1, p1; rep from * to end.

3rd row: K1, PB1, k1, *p3, k1, PB1, k1; rep from * to end.

4th row: P1, KB1, p1, *k3, pass 3rd st on right-hand needle over first 2 sts, p1, KB1, p1; rep from * to end.

Rep these 4 rows.

Diagonal Rib II

Multiple of 4.

1st and 2nd rows: *K2, p2; rep from * to end.

3rd row (right side): K1, *p2, k2; rep from * to last 3 sts, p2, k1.

4th row: P1, *k2, p2; rep from * to last 3 sts, k2, p1.

5th and 6th rows: *P2, k2; rep from * to end.

7th row: As 4th row.

8th row: As 3rd row.

Rep these 8 rows.

When working a sweater, knit both sleeves on the same needle at the same time to achieve increases that are exactly the same. This saves you from having to compare the finished sleeves.

Pyramid Triangles

Multiple of 14 + 1.

1st row (right side): K7, p1, *k13, p1; rep from * to last 7 sts, k7.

2nd and every alt row: Purl.

3rd row: K6, p3, *k11, p3; rep from * to last 6 sts, k6.

5th row: K5, p5, *k9, p5; rep from * to last 5 sts, k5.

7th row: K4, p7, *k7, p7; rep from * to last 4 sts, k4.

9th row: K3, p9, *k5, p9; rep from * to last 3 sts, k3.

11th row: K2, p11, *k3, p11; rep from * to last 2 sts, k2.

13th row: K1, *p13, k1; rep from * to end.

15th row: P1, *k13, p1; rep from * to end.

17th row: P2, k11, *p3, k11; rep from * to last 2 sts, p2.

19th row: P3, k9, *p5, k9; rep from * to last 3 sts, p3.

21st row: P4, k7, *p7, k7; rep from * to last 4 sts, p4.

23rd row: P5, k5, *p9, k5; rep from * to last 5 sts, p5.

25th row: P6, k3, *p11, k3; rep from * to last 6 sts, p6.

27th row: P7, k1, *p13, k1; rep from * to last 7 sts, p7.

28th row: Purl.

Rep these 28 rows.

Waffle Stitch

Multiple of 3 + 1.

1st row (right side): P1, *k2, p1; rep from * to end.

2nd row: K1, *p2, k1; rep from * to end.

3rd row: As 1st row.

4th row: Knit.

Rep these 4 rows.

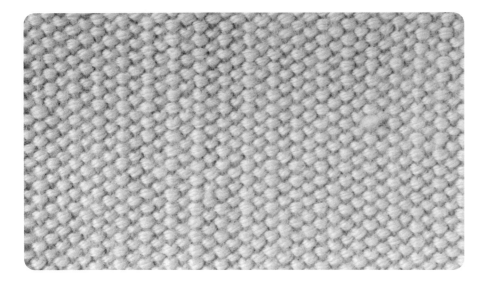

Tweed Stitch

Multiple of 2 + 1.

1st row (right side): K1, *yf, sl 1 purlwise, yb, k1; rep from
* to end.

2nd row: P2, *yb, sl 1 purlwise, yf, p1; rep from * to last st,
p1.

Rep these 2 rows.

A clever way of making knitting markers is to cut up a drink-
ing straw.

Unusual Pattern Check

Multiple of 8.

1st row (right side): Knit.

2nd row: *K4, p4; rep from * to end.

3rd row: P1, *k4, p4; rep from * to last 7 sts, k4, p3.

4th row: K2, *p4, k4; rep from * to last 6 sts, p4, k2.

5th row: P3, *k4, p4; rep from * to last 5 sts, k4, p1.

6th row: *P4, k4; rep from * to end.

7th row: Knit.

8th row: *K4, p4; rep from * to end.

Rep the last row 3 times more.

12th row: Purl.

13th row: As 6th row.

14th row: K1, *p4, k4; rep from * to last 7 sts, p4, k3.

15th row: P2, *k4, p4; rep from * to last 6 sts, k4, p2.

16th row: K3, *p4, k4; rep from * to last 5 sts, p4, k1.

17th row: As 2nd row.

18th row: Purl.

19th row: *P4, k4; rep from * to end.

Rep the last row 3 times more.

Rep these last 22 rows.

Large Basket Weave

Multiple of 6 + 2.

1st row (right side): Knit.

2nd row: Purl.

3rd row: K2, *p4, k2; rep from * to end.

4th row: P2, *k4, p2; rep from * to end.

Rep the last 2 rows once more.

7th row: Knit.

8th row: Purl.

9th row: P3, *k2, p4; rep from * to last 5 sts, k2, p3.

10th row: K3, *p2, k4; rep from * to last 5 sts, p2, k3.

Rep the last 2 rows once more.

Rep these 12 rows.

Broken Rib Diagonal

Multiple of 6.

1st row (right side): *K4, p2; rep from * to end.

2nd row: *K2, p4; rep from * to end.

3rd row: As 1st row.

4th row: As 2nd row.

5th row: K2, *p2, k4; rep from * to last 4 sts, p2, k2.

6th row: P2, *k2, p4; rep from * to last 4 sts, k2, p2.

7th row: As 5th row.

8th row: As 6th row.

9th row: *P2, k4; rep from * to end.

10th row: *P4, k2; rep from * to end.

11th row: As 9th row.

12th row: As 10th row.

Rep these 12 rows.

Small post-it notes are very handy for jotting notes, keeping track of rows, and as dividers in a loose leaf book of patterns.

Stripe Pillars

Multiple of 6 + 3.

Work 4 rows in st st, starting knit (right side).

5th row: K1, *p1, k1; rep from * to end.

6th row: P1, *k1, p1; rep from * to end.

Rep the last 2 rows once more.

9th row: K1, p1, k1, *p3, k1, p1, k1; rep from * to end.

10th row: P1, k1, p1, *k3, p1, k1, p1; rep from * to end.

Rep the last 2 rows once more.

Rep these 12 rows.

Pillar Stitch 1

Multiple of 2.

1st row (wrong side): Purl.

2nd row: K1, *yo, k2, pass yo over k2; rep from * to last st, k1.

Rep these 2 rows.

Horizontal Dash Stitch

Multiple of 10 + 6.

1st row (right side): P6, *k4, p6; rep from * to end.

2nd and every alt row: Purl.

3rd row: Knit.

5th row: P1, *k4, p6; rep from * to last 5 sts, k4, p1.

7th row: Knit.

8th row: Purl.

Rep these 8 rows.

Piqué Rib

Multiple of 10 + 3.

1st row (right side): K3, *p3, k1, p3, k3; rep from * to end.

2nd row: P3, *k3, p1, k3, p3; rep from * to end.

3rd row: As 1st row.

4th row: Knit.

Rep these 4 rows.

When you need to store your knitting, take a cork and stick the end of the needle into it to prevent stitches from slipping off.

Fancy Chevron

Multiple of 22 + 1.

1st row (right side): K1, *p3, [k1, p1] twice, k1, p5, k1, [p1, k1] twice, p3, k1; rep from * to end.

2nd row: P2, *k3, [p1, k1] twice, p1, k3, p1, [k1, p1] twice, k3, p3; rep from * to last 21 sts, k3, [p1, k1] twice, p1, k3, p1, [k1, p1] twice, k3, p2.

3rd row: K3, *p3, [k1, p1] 5 times, k1, p3, k5; rep from * to last 20 sts, p3, [k1, p1] 5 times, k1, p3, k3.

4th row: K1, *p3, k3, [p1, k1] 4 times, p1, k3, p3, k1; rep from * to end.

5th row: P2, *k3, p3, [k1, p1] 3 times, k1, p3, k3, p3; rep from * to last 21 sts, k3, p3, [k1, p1] 3 times, k1, p3, k3, p2.

6th row: K3, *p3, k3, [p1, k1] twice, p1, k3, p3, k5; rep from * to last 20 sts, p3, k3, [p1, k1] twice, p1, k3, p3, k3.

7th row: K1, *p3, k3, p3, k1, p1, k1, p3, k3, p3, k1; rep from * to end.

8th row: K1, *[p1, k3, p3, k3] twice, p1, k1; rep from * to end.

9th row: K1, *p1, k1, p3, k3, p5, k3, p3, k1, p1, k1; rep from * to end.

10th row: K1, *p1, k1, p1, [k3, p3] twice, k3, [p1, k1] twice; rep from * to end.

11th row: K1, [p1, k1] twice, p3, k3, p1, k3, p3, *[k1, p1] 4 times, k1, p3, k3, p1, k3, p3; rep from * to last 5 sts, [k1, p1] twice, k1.

12th row: K1, [p1, k1] twice, p1, k3, p5, k3, *[p1, k1] 5 times, p1, k3, p5, k3; rep from * to last 6 sts, [p1, k1] 3 times.

13th row: P2, *[k1, p1] twice, k1, p3, k3, p3, [k1, p1] twice, k1, p3; rep from * to last 21 sts, [k1, p1] twice, k1, p3, k3, p3, [k1, p1] twice, k1, p2.

14th row: K3, *[p1, k1] twice, [p1, k3] twice, [p1, k1] twice, p1, k5; rep from * to last 20 sts, [p1, k1] twice, [p1, k3] twice, [p1, k1] twice, p1, k3.

Rep these 14 rows.

Diamond Panels

Multiple of 8 + 1.

1st row (right side): Knit.

2nd row: K1, *p7, k1; rep from * to end.

3rd row: K4, *p1, k7; rep from * to last 5 sts, p1, k4.

4th row: K1, *p2, k1, p1, k1, p2, k1; rep from * to end.

5th row: K2, *[p1, k1] twice, p1, k3; rep from * to last 7 sts, [p1, k1] twice, p1, k2.

6th row: As 4th row.

7th row: As 3rd row.

8th row: As 2nd row.

Rep these 8 rows.

Slip Stitch Rib

Multiple of 2 + 1.

1st row (wrong side): Purl.

2nd row: K1, *yf, sl 1 purlwise, yb, k1; rep from * to end.

Rep these 2 rows.

If binding off annoys you, try binding off with a crochet hook in your right hand instead of a knitting needle.

Textured Tiles

Multiple of 10 + 6.

1st row (right side): P1, *k4, p1; rep from * to end.

2nd row: K1, *p4, k1; rep from * to end.

Rep the last 2 rows once more, then 1st row again.

6th row: K6, *p4, k6; rep from * to end.

7th row: As 1st row.

Rep the last 2 rows twice more.

12th row: As 2nd row.

13th row: As 1st row.

Rep the last 2 rows once more.

16th row: K1, p4, *k6, p4; rep from * to last st, k1.

17th row: As 1st row.

Rep the last 2 rows once more, then 16th row again.

Rep these 20 rows.

Bobble Rib

Multiple of 8 + 3.

1st row (right side): K3, *p2, [p1, k1] twice into next st, pass the first 3 of these sts, one at a time, over the 4th st (bobble made), p2, k3; rep from * to end.

2nd row: P3, *k2, p1, k2, p3; rep from * to end.

3rd row: K3, *p2, k1, p2, k3; rep from * to end.

4th row: As 2nd row.

Rep these 4 rows.

Berry Trellis

Multiple of 12 + 7.

1st row (right side): K3, p1, k3, *p2, k1, p2, k3, p1, k3; rep from * to end.

2nd row: P3, k1, p3, *k2, p1, k2, p3, k1, p3; rep from * to end.

3rd row: K2, p1, k1, p1, k2, *p2, k1, p2, k2, p1, k1, p1, k2; rep from * to end.

4th row: P2, k1, p1, k1, p2, *k2, p1, k2, p2, k1, p1, k1, p2; rep from * to end.

5th row: K1, [p1, k1] 3 times, *[p2, k1] twice, [p1, k1] 3 times; rep from * to end.

6th row: P1, [k1, p1] 3 times, *[k2, p1] twice, [k1, p1] 3 times; rep from * to end.

7th and 8th rows: As 3rd and 4th rows.

9th and 10th rows: As 1st and 2nd rows.

11th row: [K1, p2] twice, *k3, p1, k3, p2, k1, p2; rep from * to last st, k1.

12th row: [P1, k2] twice, *p3, k1, p3, k2, p1, k2; rep from * to last st, p1.

13th row: [K1, p2] twice, *k2, p1, k1, p1, k2, p2, k1, p2; rep from * to last st, k1.

14th row: [P1, k2] twice, *p2, k1, p1, k1, p2, k2, p1, k2; rep from * to last st, p1.

15th row: [K1, p2] twice, k1, *[p1, k1] 3 times, [p2, k1] twice; rep from * to end.

16th row: [P1, k2] twice, p1, *[k1, p1] 3 times, [k2, p1] twice; rep from * to end.

17th and 18th rows: As 13th and 14th rows.

19th and 20th rows: As 11th and 12th rows.

Rep these 20 rows.

Enlarged Basket Stitch

Multiple of 18 + 10.

1st row (right side): K11, *p2, k2, p2, k12; rep from * to last 17 sts, p2, k2, p2, k11.

2nd row: P1, *k8, [p2, k2] twice, p2; rep from * to last 9 sts, k8, p1.

3rd row: K1, *p8, [k2, p2] twice, k2; rep from * to last 9 sts, p8, k1.

4th row: P11, *k2, p2, k2, p12; rep from * to last 17 sts, k2, p2, k2, p11.

Rep the last 4 rows once more.

9th row: Knit.

10th row: [P2, k2] twice, p12, *k2, p2, k2, p12; rep from * to last 8 sts, [k2, p2] twice.

11th row: [K2, p2] twice, k2, *p8, [k2, p2] twice, k2; rep from * to end.

12th row: [P2, k2] twice, p2, *k8, [p2, k2] twice, p2; rep from * to end.

13th row: [K2, p2] twice, k12, *p2, k2, p2, k12; rep from * to last 8 sts, [p2, k2] twice.

Rep the last 4 rows once more.

18th row: Purl.

Rep these 18 rows.

Garter and Slip Stitch

Multiple of 6 + 4.

1st row (right side): Knit.

2nd row: K1, *yf, sl 2 purlwise, yb, k4; rep from * to last 3 sts, yf, sl2 purlwise, yb, k1.

3rd row: K1, *keeping yarn at back sl 2 purlwise, k4; rep from * to last 3 sts, sl 2 purlwise, k1.

Rep the last 2 rows once more.

6th row: As 2nd row.

7th row: Knit.

8th row: K4, *yf, sl 2 purlwise, yb, k4; rep from * to end.

9th row: K4, *keeping yarn at back sl 2 purlwise, k4; rep from * to end.

Rep the last 2 rows once more.

12th row: As 8th row.

Rep these 12 rows.

Granite Rib

Multiple of 8 + 2.

1st row (right side): K2, *[C2F] 3 times, k2; rep from * to end.

2nd row: Purl.

3rd row: K2, *[knit 3rd st from left-hand needle, then 2nd st, then 1st stitch, slipping all 3 sts off needle together] twice, k2; rep from * to end.

4th row: Purl.

Rep these 4 rows.

Use a long straight knitting needle to baste seams together when sewing up.

Chevron

Multiple of 8 + 1.

1st row (right side): K1, *p7, k1; rep from * to end.

2nd row: P1, *k7, p1; rep from * to end.

3rd row: K2, *p5, k3; rep from * to last 7 sts, p5, k2.

4th row: P2, *k5, p3; rep from * to last 7 sts, k5, p2.

5th row: K3, *p3, k5; rep from * to last 6 sts, p3, k3.

6th row: P3, *k3, p5; rep from * to last 6 sts, k3, p3.

7th row: K4, *p1, k7; rep from * to last 5 sts, p1, k4.

8th row: P4, *k1, p7; rep from * to last 5 sts, k1, p4.

9th row: As 2nd row.

10th row: As 1st row.

11th row: As 4th row.

12th row: As 3rd row.

13th row: As 6th row.

14th row: As 5th row.

15th row: As 8th row.

16th row: As 7th row.

Rep these 16 rows.

Intertwined Texture Stitch

Multiple of 15 + 2.

1st row (right side): *P13, k2; rep from * to last 2 sts, p2.

2nd row: K2, *p2, k13; rep from * to end.

3rd row: As 1st row.

4th row: Purl.

5th row: P2, *k2, p1, [k1, p1] 4 times, k2, p2; rep from * to end.

6th row: K2, *p3, k1, [p1, k1] 3 times, p3, k2; rep from * to end.

Rep the last 2 rows 4 times more.

15th row: P2, *k2, p13; rep from * to end.

16th row: *K13, p2; rep from * to last 2 sts, k2.

17th row: As 15th row.

18th row: Purl.

Rep these 18 rows.

Garter Stitch Diamonds

Multiple of 8 + 2.

1st row (right side): Knit.

2nd row: P4, *keeping yarn at front sl 2 purlwise, p6; rep from * to last 6 sts, sl 2 purlwise, p4.

3rd row: K3, *C2F, C2B, k4; rep from * to last 7 sts, C2F, C2B, k3.

4th row: P3, *keeping yarn at front sl 1 purlwise, yb, k2, yf, sl 1 purlwise, p4; rep from * to last 7 sts, sl 1 purlwise, yb, k2, yf, sl 1 purlwise, p3.

5th row: K2, *C2F, k2, C2B, k2; rep from * to end.

6th row: P2, *keeping yarn at front sl 1 purlwise, yb, k4, yf, sl 1 purlwise, p2; rep from * to end.

7th row: K1, *C2F, k4, C2B; rep from * to last st, k1.

8th row: P1, keeping yarn at front sl 1 purlwise, yb, *k6, yf, sl 2 purlwise, yb; rep from * to last 8 sts, k6, yf, sl 1 purlwise, p1.

9th row: Knit.

10th row: As 8th row.

11th row: K1, *C2B, k4, C2F; rep from * to last st, k1.

12th row: As 6th row.

13th row: K2, *C2B, k2, C2F, k2; rep from * to end.

14th row: As 4th row.

15th row: K3, *C2B, C2F, k4; rep from * to last 7 sts, C2B, C2F, k3.

16th row: As 2nd row.

Rep these 16 rows.

Basket Weave Rib

Multiple of 15 + 8.

1st row (right side): *P3, k2, p3, k1, [C2F] 3 times; rep from * to last 8 sts, p3, k2, p3.

2nd row: *K3, purl into 2nd st on needle, then purl first st slipping both sts off needle together (called C2P), k3, p1, [C2P] 3 times; rep from * to last 8 sts, k3, C2P, k3.

Rep these 2 rows.

Garter Stitch Ridges

Any number of stitches.

1st row (right side): Knit.

2nd row: Purl.

Rep the last 2 rows once more.

Purl 6 rows.

Rep these 10 rows.

For those who like to knit on the go, photocopying the pattern makes for a lighter load and takes up less room in your bag.

Ladder Tile

Multiple of 12.

1st row (right side): K4, p1, *k11, p1; rep from * to last 7 sts, k7.

2nd and every alt row: Purl.

3rd and 5th rows: K4, p2, *k10, p2; rep from * to last 6 sts, k6.

7th row: K4, p7, *k5, p7; rep from * to last st, k1.

9th row: *K4, p8; rep from * to end.

11th row: K1, p7, *k5, p7; rep from * to last 4 sts, k4.

13th row: *P8, k4; rep from * to end.

15th and 17th rows: K6, p2, *k10, p2; rep from * to last 4 sts, k4.

19th row: K7, p1, *k11, p1; rep from * to last 4 sts, k4.

20th row: Purl.

Rep these 20 rows.

Bamboo Stitch

Multiple of 14 + 9.

1st and every alt row (right side): P2, *k5, p2; rep from * to end.

2nd row: K9, *p5, k9; rep from * to end.

4th row: K2, *p5, k2; rep from * to end.

6th row: K2, p5, *k9, p5; rep from * to last 2 sts, k2.

8th row: As 4th row.

Rep these 8 rows.

Spiral Rib

Multiple of 6 + 3.

1st row (right side): K3, *p3, k3; rep from * to end.

2nd row: P3, *k3, p3; rep from * to end.

3rd row: As 1st row.

4th row: K1, *p3, k3; rep from * to last 2 sts, p2.

5th row: K2, *p3, k3; rep from * to last st, p1.

6th row: As 4th row.

7th row: As 4th row.

8th row: As 5th row.

9th row: As 4th row.

10th row: K3, *p3, k3; rep from * to end.

11th row: As 2nd row.

12th row: As 10th row.

13th row: P2, *k3, p3; rep from * to last st, k1.

14th row: P1, *k3, p3; rep from * to last 2 sts, k2.

15th row: As 13th row.

16th row: As 13th row.

17th row: As 14th row.

18th row: As 13th row.

Rep these 18 rows.

Knot Stitch 1

Multiple of 2 + 1.

1st row (right side): Knit.

2nd row: K1, *p2tog without slipping sts off needle, then k tog the same 2 sts; rep from * to end.

3rd row: Knit.

4th row: *P2tog without slipping sts off needle, then k tog the same 2 sts; rep from * to last st, k1.

Rep these 4 rows.

Dotted Chevron

Multiple of 18.

1st row (right side): K8, *p2, k16; rep from * to last 10 sts, p2, k8.

2nd row: P7, *k4, p14; rep from * to last 11 sts, k4, p7.

3rd row: P1, *k5, p2, k2, p2, k5, p2; rep from * to last 17 sts, k5, p2, k2, p2, k5, p1.

4th row: K2, *p3, k2, p4, k2, p3, k4; rep from * to last 16 sts, p3, k2, p4, k2, p3, k2.

5th row: P1, *k3, p2, k6, p2, k3, p2; rep from * to last 17 sts, k3, p2, k6, p2, k3, p1.

6th row: P3, *k2, [p3, k2] twice, p6; rep from * to last 15 sts, k2, [p3, k2] twice, p3.

7th row: K2, *p2, k3, p4, k3, p2, k4; rep from * to last 16 sts, p2, k3, p4, k3, p2, k2.

8th row: P1, *k2, [p5, k2] twice, p2; rep from * to last 17 sts, k2, [p5, k2] twice, p1.

9th row: P2, *k14, p4; rep from * to last 16 sts, k14, p2.

10th row: K1, *p16, k2; rep from * to last 17 sts, p16, k1.

Rep these 10 rows.

Tweed Pattern

Multiple of 6 + 3.

1st row (right side): K3, *p3, k3; rep from * to end.

Rep the last row twice more.

4th row: Knit.

5th row: Purl.

6th row: Knit.

7th row: K3, *p3, k3; rep from * to end.

Rep the last row twice more.

10th row: Purl.

11th row: Knit.

12th row: Purl.

Rep these 12 rows.

Experiment with yarns of different textures to give a totally new characteristic to the stitch.

Optical Texture

Multiple of 24 + 2.

1st row (right side): P2, *k2, p18, k2, p2; rep from * to end.

2nd row: K2, *p2, k18, p2, k2; rep from * to end.

3rd row: P2, *k18, p2, k2, p2; rep from * to end.

4th row: K2, *p2, k2, p18, k2; rep from * to end.

5th row: P2, *k2, p14, [k2, p2] twice; rep from * to end.

6th row: *[K2, p2] twice, k14, p2; rep from * to last 2 sts, k2.

7th row: P2, k2, p2, k10, p2, *[k2, p2] 3 times, k10, p2; rep from * to last 8 sts, [k2, p2] twice.

8th row: K2, [p2, k2] twice, p10, k2, *[p2, k2] 3 times, p10, k2; rep from * to last 4 sts, p2, k2.

9th row: [P2, k2] twice, p6, k2, *[p2, k2] 4 times, p6, k2; rep from * to last 10 sts, p2, [k2, p2] twice.

10th row: [K2, p2] 3 times, k6, *p2, [k2, p2] 4 times, k6; rep from * to last 8 sts, [p2, k2] twice.

11th row: P2, *k2, p2; rep from * to end.

12th row: K2, *p2, k2; rep from * to end.

13th row: [P2, k2] 3 times, p6, k2, *[p2, k2] 4 times, p6, k2; rep from * to last 6 sts, p2, k2, p2.

14th row: [K2, p2] twice, k6 *p2, [k2, p2] 4 times, k6; rep from * to last 12 sts, [p2, k2] 3 times.

15th row: P2, [k2, p2] twice, k10, p2, *[k2, p2] 3 times, k10, p2; rep from * to last 4 sts, k2, p2.

16th row: K2, p2, k2, p10, k2, *[p2, k2] 3 times, p10, k2; rep from * to last 8 sts, [p2, k2] twice.

17th row: *[P2, k2] twice, p14, k2; rep from * to last 2 sts, p2.

18th row: K2, p2, k14, p2, *[k2, p2] twice, k14, p2; rep from * to last 6 sts, k2, p2, k2.

19th row: P2, *k2, p2, k18, p2; rep from * to end.

20th row: K2, *p18, k2, p2, k2; rep from * to end.

Rep these 20 rows.

Chain Stitch Rib

Multiple of 3 + 2.

1st row (wrong side): K2, *p1, k2; rep from * to end.

2nd row: P2, *k1, p2; rep from * to end.

3rd row: As 1st row.

4th row: P2, *yb, insert needle through center of st 3 rows below next st on needle and knit this in the usual way, slipping st above off needle at the same time, p2; rep from * to end.

Rep these 4 rows.

Diamond Pattern

Multiple of 8 + 1.

1st row (right side): P1, *k7, p1; rep from * to end.

2nd row: K2, p5, *k3, p5; rep from * to last 2 sts, k2.

3rd row: K1, *p2, k3, p2, k1; rep from * to end.

4th row: P2, k2, p1, k2, *p3, k2, p1, k2; rep from * to last 2 sts, p2.

5th row: K3, p3, *k5, p3; rep from * to last 3 sts, k3.

6th row: P4, k1, *p7, k1; rep from * to last 4 sts, p4.

7th row: As 5th row.

8th row: As 4th row.

9th row: As 3rd row.

10th row: As 2nd row.

Rep these 10 rows.

Brick Stitch 1

Multiple of 4 + 1.

1st row (right side): K4, *k1 winding yarn twice round needle, k3; rep from * to last st, k1.

2nd row: P4, *sl 1 purlwise dropping extra loop, p3; rep from * to last st, p1.

3rd row: K4, *sl 1 purlwise, k3; rep from * to last st, k1.

4th row: K4, *yf, sl 1 purlwise, yb, k3; rep from * to last st, k1.

5th row: K2, *k1 winding yarn twice round needle, k3; rep from * to last 3 sts, k1 winding yarn twice round needle, k2.

6th row: P2, *sl 1 purlwise dropping extra loop, p3; rep from * to last 3 sts, sl 1 purlwise, p2.

7th row: K2, *sl 1 purlwise, k3; rep from * to last 3 sts, sl 1 purlwise, k2.

8th row: K2, *yf, sl 1 purlwise, yb, k3; rep from * to last 3 sts, yf, sl 1 purlwise, yb, k2.

Rep these 8 rows.

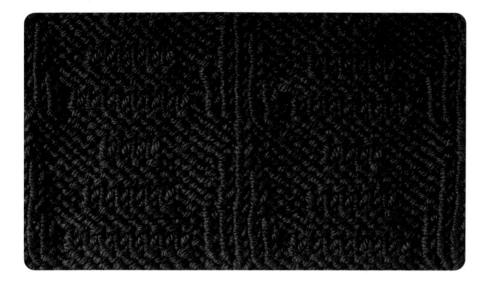

Pyramids II

Multiple of 8 + 1.

1st row (wrong side): P1, *k1, p1; rep from * to end.

2nd row: K1, *p1, k1; rep from * to end.

Rep these 2 rows once more.

5th row: P2, *[k1, p1] twice, k1, p3; rep from * to last 7 sts, [k1, p1] twice, k1, p2.

6th row: K2, *[p1, k1] twice, p1, k3; rep from * to last 7 sts, [p1, k1] twice, p1, k2.

Rep the last 2 rows once more.

9th row: P3, *k1, p1, k1, p5; rep from * to last 6 sts, k1, p1, k1, p3.

10th row: K3, *p1, k1, p1, k5; rep from * to last 6 sts, p1, k1, p1, k3.

Rep the last 2 rows once more.

13th row: P4, *k1, p7; rep from * to last 5 sts, k1, p4.

14th row: K4, *p1, k7; rep from * to last 5 sts, p1, k4.

Rep the last 2 rows once more.

Rep these 16 rows.

Mock Cable Rib

Multiple of 7 + 2.

1st row (right side): P2, *C2B, k3, p2; rep from * to end.

2nd and every alt row: K2, *p5, k2; rep from * to end.

3rd row: P2, *k1, C2B, k2, p2; rep from * to end.

5th row: P2, *k2, C2B, k1, p2; rep from * to end.

7th row: P2, *k3, C2B, p2; rep from * to end.

8th row: K2, *p5, k2; rep from * to end.

Rep these 8 rows.

When threading beads, dab a little clear nail polish on the end of the yarn. This causes the yarn to stiffen and makes it easy to thread. It works particularly well with beads with small openings.

Zigzag Stitch

Multiple of 6 sts.

1st row (right side): *K3, p3; rep from * to end.

2nd and every alt row: Purl.

3rd row: P1, *k3, p3; rep from * to last 5 sts, k3, p2.

5th row: P2, *k3, p3; rep from * to last 4 sts, k3, p1.

7th row: *P3, k3; rep from * to end.

9th row: As 5th row.

11th row: As 3rd row.

12th row: Purl.

Rep these 12 rows.

Garter Drop Stitch

Any number of stitches.

Work 4 rows in garter stitch (every row knit).

5th row: *K1 winding yarn twice round needle; rep from * to end.

6th row: K to end, dropping the extra loops.

Rep these 6 rows.

Country Grove

Multiple of 6 + 3.

1st and every alt row (right side): Knit.

2nd row: Knit.

4th and 6th rows: P3, *k3, p3; rep from * to end.

8th and 10th rows: Knit.

12th and 14th rows: K3, *p3, k3; rep from * to end.

16th row: Knit.

Rep these 16 rows.

Spaced Checks

Multiple of 10 + 1.

1st row (wrong side): Purl.

2nd row: K4, *p3, k7; rep from * to last 7 sts, p3, k4.

3rd row: P4, *k3, p7; rep from * to last 7 sts, k3, p4.

4th row: As 2nd row.

5th row: Purl.

6th row: Knit.

7th row: K2, *p7, k3; rep from * to last 9 sts, p7, k2.

8th row: P2, *k7, p3; rep from * to last 9 sts, k7, p2.

9th row: As 7th row.

10th row: Knit.

Rep these 10 rows.

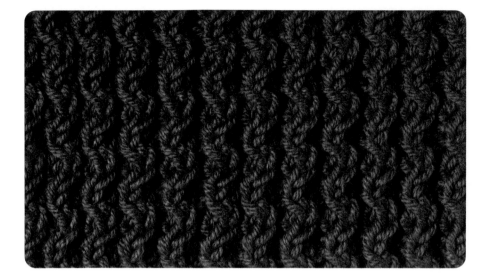

Wavy Rib

Multiple of 3 + 1.

1st row (wrong side): K1, *p2, k1; rep from * to end.

2nd row: P1, *C2F, p1; rep from * to end.

3rd row: As 1st row.

4th row: P1, *C2B, p1; rep from * to end.

Rep these 4 rows.

Experiment with different needle sizes. This can often create an unexpected dynamic and prompt further inspiration for a project or design.

Ridged Knot Stitch 1

Multiple of 3 + 2.

1st row (right side): Knit.

2nd row: K1, *p3tog leaving sts on needle, yrn, then p same 3 sts together again; rep from * to last st, k1.

3rd and 4th rows: Knit.

Rep these 4 rows.

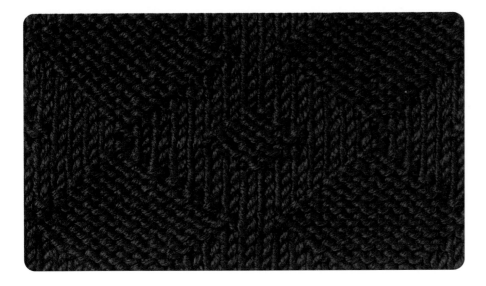

Fancy Diamond Pattern

Multiple of 15.

1st row (right side): K1, *p13, k2; rep from * to last 14 sts, p13, k1.

2nd row: P2, *k11, p4; rep from * to last 13 sts, k11, p2.

3rd row: K3, *p9, k6; rep from * to last 12 sts, p9, k3.

4th row: P4, *k7, p8; rep from * to last 11 sts, k7, p4.

5th row: K5, *p5, k10; rep from * to last 10 sts, p5, k5.

6th row: K1, *p5, k3, p5, k2; rep from * to last 14 sts, p5, k3, p5, k1.

7th row: P2, *k5, p1, k5, p4; rep from * to last 13 sts, k5, p1,
k5, p2.

8th row: As 3rd row.

9th row: As 7th row.

10th row: As 6th row.

11th row: As 5th row.

12th row: As 4th row.

13th row: As 3rd row.

14th row: As 2nd row.

Rep these 14 rows.

Slanted Bamboo

Multiple of 8.

1st row (right side): P1, k6, *p2, k6; rep from * to last st, p1.

2nd row: K1, p5, *k3, p5; rep from * to last 2 sts, k2.

3rd row: P3, k4, *p4, k4; rep from * to last st, p1.

4th row: K1, p3, k2, p1, *k2, p3, k2, p1; rep from * to last st, k1.

5th row: P1, k2, *p2, k2; rep from * to last st, p1.

6th row: K1, p1, k2, p3, *k2, p1, k2, p3; rep from * to last st, k1.

7th row: P1, k4, *p4, k4; rep from * to last 3 sts, p3.

8th row: K2, p5, *k3, p5; rep from * to last st, k1.

9th row: As 1st row.

10th row: K1, p6, *k2, p6; rep from * to last st, k1.

Rep these 10 rows.

Square Rib

Multiple of 2 + 1.

1st row (right side): K2, p1, *k1, p1; rep from * to last 2 sts, k2.

2nd row: K1, *p1, k1; rep from * to end.

3rd row: As 1st row.

4th row: K1, p1, *yb, insert needle through centre of st 2 rows below next st on needle and knit this in the usual way slipping st above off needle at the same time, p1; rep from * to last st, k1.

Rep these 4 rows.

Diagonal Knot Stitch 1

Multiple of 3 + 1.

Special Abbreviation: Make Knot = P3tog leaving sts on needle, yrn, then purl same 3 sts together again.

1st and every alt row (right side): Knit.

2nd row: *Make Knot (see Special Abbreviation); rep from * to last st, p1.

4th row: P2, *Make Knot; rep from * to last 2 sts, p2.

6th row: P1, *Make Knot; rep from * to end.

Rep these 6 rows.

Take inspiration from other textiles for stitches—waffles, semi-plains, herringbones, dobbys, seersucker, prints, wovens, etc. They may be present in your room or around you already.

Close Checks

Multiple of 6 + 3.

1st row (right side): K3, *p3, k3; rep from * to end.

2nd row: P3, *k3, p3; rep from * to end.

Rep the last 2 rows once more.

5th row: As 2nd row.

6th row: As 1st row.

Rep the last 2 rows once more.

Rep these 8 rows.

Mock Cable – Left

Multiple of 4 + 2.

1st row (right side): P2, *k2, p2; rep from * to end.

2nd row: K2, *p2, k2; rep from * to end.

3rd row: P2, *C2B, p2; rep from * to end.

4th row: As 2nd row.

Rep these 4 rows.

Berry Ladder

Multiple of 20 + 10.

1st row (right side): P2, *k2, p2; rep from * to end.

2nd row: K2, *p2, k2; rep from * to end.

3rd row: [K2, p2] twice, *k4, p2, k2, p2; rep from * to last 2 sts, k2.

4th row: [P2, k2] twice, *p4, k2, p2, k2; rep from * to last 2 sts, p2.

Rep the last 4 rows once more, then 1st and 2nd rows again.

11th row: As 2nd row.

12th row: P2, *k2, p2; rep from * to end.

13th row: [K2, p2] 3 times, [k4, p2] twice, *[k2, p2] twice, [k4, p2] twice; rep from * to last 6 sts, k2, p2, k2.

14th row: [P2, k2] twice, *[p4, k2] twice, [p2, k2] twice; rep from * to last 2 sts, p2.

Rep the last 4 rows once more, then 11th and 12th rows again.

Rep these 20 rows.

Embossed Lozenge Stitch

Multiple of 8 + 1.

1st row (right side): P3, *KB1, p1, KB1, p5; rep from * to last 6 sts, KB1, p1, KB1, p3.

2nd row: K3, *PB1, k1, PB1, k5; rep from * to last 6 sts, PB1, k1, PB1, k3.

Rep the last 2 rows once more.

5th row: P2, *KB1, p3; rep from * to last 3 sts, KB1, p2.

6th row: K2, *PB1, k3; rep from * to last 3 sts, PB1, k2.

7th row: P1, *KB1, p5, KB1, p1; rep from * to end.

8th row: K1, *PB1, k5, PB1, k1; rep from * to end.

9th row: As 7th row.

10th row: As 8th row.

11th row: As 5th row.

12th row: As 6th row.

Rep these 12 rows.

Single Eyelet Rib

Multiple of 5 + 2.

1st row (right side): P2, *k3, p2; rep from * to end.

2nd and every alt row: K2, *p3, k2; rep from * to end.

3rd row: P2, *k2tog, yo, k1, p2; rep from * to end.

5th row: As 1st row.

7th row: P2, *k1, yo, sl 1, k1, psso, p2; rep from * to end.

8th row: As 2nd row.

Rep these 8 rows.

Squares

Multiple of 10 + 2.

1st row (right side): Knit.

2nd row: Purl.

3rd row: K2, *p8, k2; rep from * to end.

4th row: P2, *k8, p2; rep from * to end.

5th row: K2, *p2, k4, p2, k2; rep from * to end.

6th row: P2, *k2, p4, k2, p2; rep from * to end.

Rep the last 2 rows twice more.

11th row: As 3rd row.

12th row: As 4th row.

Rep these 12 rows.

I often work a 6 row border of garter stitch at the bottom and top of my gauge swatch and a 3 stitch garter stitch border at the beginning and end of the swatch. This keeps the swatch flat but also easily to store way for future reference or use.

Crossroads

Multiple of 12 + 2.

1st row (right side): K4, p6, *k6, p6; rep from * to last 4 sts, k4.

2nd row: P4, k6, *p6, k6; rep from * to last 4 sts, p4.

3rd row: K2, *p2, k6, p2, k2; rep from * to end.

4th row: P2, *k2, p6, k2, p2; rep from * to end.

Rep the last 2 rows 3 times more.

11th and 12th rows: As 1st and 2nd rows.

13th row: Knit

14th row: Purl.

Rep these 14 rows.

Triangle Ribs

Multiple of 8.

1st row (right side): *P2, k6; rep from * to end.

2nd row: *P6, k2; rep from * to end.

3rd row: *P3, k5; rep from * to end.

4th row: *P4, k4; rep from * to end.

5th row: *P5, k3; rep from * to end.

6th row: *P2, k6; rep from * to end.

7th row: *P7, k1; rep from * to end.

8th row: *P2, k6; rep from * to end.

9th row: As 5th row.

10th row: As 4th row.

11th row: As 3rd row.

12th row: As 2nd row.

Rep these 12 rows.

Ocean Wave

Multiple of 12 + 1.

1st and every alt row (right side): Knit.

2nd row: P5, k3, *p9, k3; rep from * to last 5 sts, p5.

4th row: P4, k5, *p7, k5; rep from * to last 4 sts, p4.

6th row: P3, k3, p1, k3, *p5, k3, p1, k3; rep from * to last 3 sts, p3.

8th row: P2, k3, *p3, k3; rep from * to last 2 sts, p2.

10th row: P1, *k3, p5, k3, p1; rep from * to end.

12th row: Purl.

Rep these 12 rows.

Elongated Chevron

Multiple of 18 + 1.

1st row (right side): P1, *[k2, p2] twice, k1, [p2, k2] twice, p1; rep from * to end.

2nd row: K1, *[p2, k2] twice, p1, [k2, p2] twice, k1; rep from * to end.

Rep the last 2 rows once more.

5th row: [P2, k2] twice, *p3, k2, p2, k2; rep from * to last 2 sts, p2.

6th row: [K2, p2] twice, *k3, p2, k2, p2; rep from * to last 2 sts, k2.

Rep the last 2 rows once more.

9th row: As 2nd row.

10th row: As 1st row.

11th row: As 2nd row.

12th row: As 1st row.

13th row: As 6th row.

14th row: As 5th row.

15th row: As 6th row.

16th row: As 5th row.

Rep these 16 rows.

Double Eyelet Rib

Multiple of 7 + 2.

1st row (right side): P2, *k5, p2; rep from * to end.

2nd row: K2, *p5, k2; rep from * to end.

3rd row: P2, *k2tog, yo, k1, yo, sl 1, k1, psso, p2; rep from *
to end.

4th row: As 2nd row.

Rep these 4 rows.

Moss Stitch Zigzag

Multiple of 9.

1st row (right side): *[K1, p1] twice, k4, p1; rep from * to end.

2nd row: *P4, [k1, p1] twice, k1; rep from * to end.

3rd row: [K1, p1] 3 times, *k4, [p1, k1] twice, p1; rep from * to last 3 sts, k3.

4th row: P2, *[k1, p1] twice, k1, p4; rep from * to last 7 sts, [k1, p1] twice, k1, p2.

5th row: K3, *[p1, k1] twice, p1, k4; rep from * to last 6 sts, [p1, k1] 3 times.

6th row: *[K1, p1] twice, k1, p4; rep from * to end.

7th row: As 5th row.

8th row: As 4th row.

9th row: As 3rd row.

10th row: As 2nd row.

Rep these 10 rows.

Mock Ribbing

Multiple of 2 + 1.

1st row (right side): K1, *p1, k1; rep from * to end.

2nd row: P1, *keeping yarn at front of work sl 1 purlwise, p1; rep from * to end.

Rep these 2 rows.

Hollow Crosses

Multiple of 18 + 12.

1st row (right side): Knit.

2nd row: Purl.

3rd row: K4, p4, *k14, p4; rep from * to last 4 sts, k4.

4th row: P4, k4, *p14, k4; rep from * to last 4 sts, p4.

Rep the last 2 rows once more.

7th row: P4, k4, p4, *k6, p4, k4, p4; rep from * to end.

8th row: K4, p4, k4, *p6, k4, p4, k4; rep from * to end.

Rep the last 2 rows once more.

11th and 12th rows: As 3rd and 4th rows.

Rep the last 2 rows once more.

15th row: Knit.

16th row: Purl.

17th row: K13, p4, *k14, p4; rep from * to last 13 sts, k13.

18th row: P13, k4, *p14, k4; rep from * to last 13sts, p13.

Rep the last 2 rows once more.

21st row: P3, k6, *p4, k4, p4, k6; rep from * to last 3 sts, p3.

22nd row: K3, p6, *k4, p4, k4, p6; rep from * to last 3 sts, k3.

Rep the last 2 rows once more.

25th and 26th rows: As 17th and 18th rows.

Rep the last 2 rows once more.

Rep these 28 rows.

Textured Stripe

Multiple of 3.

1st row (right side): Knit.

2nd row: Purl.

Rep the last 2 rows once more.

5th row: K1, *p1, k2; rep from * to last 2 sts, p1, k1.

6th row: P1, *k1, p2; rep from * to last 2 sts, k1, p1.

Rep the last 2 rows once more.

9th row: *P2, k1; rep from * to end.

10th row: *P1, k2; rep from * to end.

Rep the last 2 rows once more.

Rep these 12 rows.

Little Hour Glass Ribbing

Multiple of 4 + 2.

Note: Sts should not be counted after 3rd row.

1st row (wrong side): K2, *p2, k2; rep from * to end.

2nd row: P2, *k2tog tbl, then knit same 2 sts tog through front loops, p2; rep from * to end.

3rd row: K2, *p1, yrn, p1, k2; rep from * to end.

4th row: P2, *yb, sl 1, k1, psso, k1, p2; rep from * to end.

Rep these 4 rows.

Simple lace and eyelet patterns can be created by using combinations of knit and purl stitches—Little Hour Glass Ribbing (this page) and 'Faggotted Rib' (page 238) are examples of this.

Polperro Laughing Boy

Multiple of 6.

1st row (right side): Knit.

2nd row: P2, k2, *p4, k2; rep from * to last 2 sts, p2.

Rep these 2 rows once more.

Work 4 rows in st st, starting knit.

Rep these 8 rows.

Dash Stitch

Multiple of 6 + 1.

1st row (wrong side): K3, *PB1, k5; rep from * to last 4 sts, PB1, k3.

2nd row: P3, *KB1, p5; rep from * to last 4 sts, KB1, p3.

Rep these 2 rows twice more.

7th row: *PB1, k5; rep from * to last st, PB1.

8th row: *KB1, p5; rep from * to last st, KB1.

Rep these 2 rows twice more.

Rep these 12 rows.

Fisherman's Rib

Note: Each set of instructions gives the same appearance but a different 'feel'. For example (C) is a firmer fabric than (A).

(A) Multiple of 2 + 1.

Foundation row: Knit.

1st row (right side): Sl 1, *K1B, p1; rep from * to end.

2nd row: Sl 1, *p1, K1B; rep from * to last 2 sts, p1, k1.

Rep the last 2 rows only.

(B) Multiple of 2 + 1.

Foundation row: Knit.

1st row (right side): Sl 1, *K1B, k1; rep from * to end.

2nd row: Sl 1, *k1, K1B; rep from * to last 2 sts, k2.

Rep the last 2 rows only.

(C) Multiple of 3 + 1.

1st row (right side): Sl 1, *k2tog, yfon, sl 1 purlwise; rep from * to last 3 sts, k2tog, k1.

2nd row: Sl 1, *yfon, sl 1 purlwise, k2tog (the yfon and sl 1 of previous row); rep from * to last 2 sts, yfon, sl 1 purlwise, k1.

Rep the last 2 rows.

Vine Cross

Multiple of 20 + 1.

1st row (right side): K6, p9, *k11, p9; rep from * to last 6 sts, k6.

2nd row: P5, k11, *p9, k11; rep from * to last 5 sts, p5.

3rd row: K4, p13, *k7, p13; rep from * to last 4 sts, k4.

4th row: P3, k4, p7, k4, *p5, k4, p7, k4; rep from * to last 3 sts, p3.

5th row: K3, p3, k9, p3, *k5, p3, k9, p3; rep from * to last 3 sts, k3.

6th row: P3, k2, p11, k2, *p5, k2, p11, k2; rep from * to last 3 sts, p3.

7th row: K3, p1, k13, p1, *k5, p1, k13, p1; rep from * to last 3 sts, k3.

8th row: As 3rd row.

9th row: As 2nd row.

10th row: K6, p9, *k11, p9; rep from * to last 6 sts, k6.

11th row: K3, p4, k7, p4, *k5, p4, k7, p4; rep from * to last 3 sts, k3.

12th row: P4, k3, *p7, k3; rep from * to last 4 sts, p4.

13th row: K5, p2, k7, p2, *k9, p2, k7, p2; rep from * to last 5 sts, k5.

14th row: P6, k1, p7, k1, *p11, k1, p7, k1; rep from * to last 6 sts, p6.

Rep these 14 rows.

Doubled Ridged Rib

Multiple of 2 + 1.

1st and 2nd rows: Knit.

3rd row (right side): P1, *k1, p1; rep from * to end.

4th row: K1, *p1, k1; rep from * to end.

5th and 6th rows: Knit.

7th row: As 4th row.

8th row: P1, *k1, p1; rep from * to end.

Rep these 8 rows.

Diagonal March

Multiple of 6 + 2.

1st row (right side): P2, *k4, p2; rep from * to end.

2nd row: K2, *p4, k2; rep from * to end.

Rep the last 2 rows 3 times more.

9th row: K1, *p2, k4; rep from * to last st, p1.

10th row: *P4, k2; rep from * to last 2 sts, p2.

11th row: K3, p2, *k4, p2; rep from * to last 3 sts, k3.

12th row: P2, *k2, p4; rep from * to end.

13th row: P1, *k4, p2; rep from * to last st, k1.

14th, 15th and 16th rows: As 8th, 9th and 10th rows.

17th row: As 11th row.

18th row: P3, k2, *p4, k2; rep from * to last 3 sts, p3.

Rep the last 2 rows 3 times more.

25th row: *K4, p2; rep from * to last 2 sts, k2.

26th row: P1, *k2, p4; rep from * to last st, k1.

27th row: As 1st row.

28th row: K1, *p4, k2; rep from * to last st, p1.

29th row: K2, *p2, k4; rep from * to end.

30th row: P3, k2, *p4, k2; rep from * to last 3 sts, p3.

31st row: *K4, p2; rep from * to last 2 sts, k2.

32nd row: As 26th row.

Rep these 32 rows.

Check Pattern

Multiple of 3 + 1.

1st row (right side): Knit.

2nd row: Purl.

3rd row: K1, *p2, k1; rep from * to end.

4th row: Purl.

Rep these 4 rows.

Half Fisherman's Rib

Note: Both sets of instructions give the same appearance but a different 'feel'. (B) is a firmer fabric than (A).

(A) Multiple of 2 + 1.
1st row (right side): Sl 1, knit to end.
2nd row: Sl 1, *K1B, p1; rep from * to end.
Rep these 2 rows.

(B) Multiple of 2 + 1.
1st row (right side): Sl 1, *p1, k1; rep from * to end.
2nd row: Sl 1, *K1B, p1; rep from * to end.
Rep these 2 rows.

One of my favorite stitches is simple garter stitch. Since it can be bulky, I often substitute reverse stockinette stitch, which gives a similar effect but a lighter fabric.

Bouquet Stitch

Multiple of 16 + 1.

1st row (right side): [K1, p1] twice, [k4, p1] twice, *[k1, p1] 3 times, [k4, p1] twice; rep from * to last 3 sts, k1, p1, k1.

2nd row: K1, p1, k1, p4, k3, p4, *k1, [p1, k1] twice, p4, k3, p4; rep from * to last 3 sts, k1, p1, k1.

3rd row: K1, *p1, k4, p5, k4, p1, k1; rep from * to end.

4th row: K1, *p4, k7, p4, k1; rep from * to end.

5th row: K4, p4, k1, p4, *k7, p4, k1, p4; rep from * to last 4 sts, k4.

6th row: P4, k3, p1, k1, p1, k3, *p7, k3, p1, k1, p1, k3; rep from * to last 4 sts, p4.

7th row: K4, p2, k1, [p1, k1] twice, p2, *k7, p2, k1, [p1, k1] twice, p2; rep from * to last 4 sts, k4.

8th row: P4, k1, [p1, k1] 4 times, *p7, k1, [p1, k1] 4 times; rep from * to last 4 sts, p4.

9th row: P1, k4, p1, [k1, p1] 3 times, *[k4, p1] twice, [k1, p1] 3 times; rep from * to last 5 sts, k4, p1.

10th row: K2, p4, k1, [p1, k1] twice, p4, *k3, p4, k1, [p1, k1] twice, p4; rep from * to last 2 sts, k2.

11th row: P3, k4, p1, k1, p1, k4, *p5, k4, p1, k1, p1, k4; rep from * to last 3 sts, p3.

12th row: K4, p4, k1, p4, *k7, p4, k1, p4; rep from * to last 4 sts, k4.

13th row: K1, *p4, k7, p4, k1; rep from * to end.

14th row: K1, *p1, k3, p7, k3, p1, k1; rep from * to end.

15th row: K1, p1, k1, p2, k7, p2, *k1, [p1, k1] twice, p2, k7, p2; rep from * to last 3 sts, k1, p1, k1.

16th row: K1, [p1, k1] twice, p7, k1, *[p1, k1] 4 times, p7, k1; rep from * to last 4 sts, [p1, k1] twice.

Rep these 16 rows.

Banded Basket Stitch

Multiple of 9 + 6.

1st row (right side): P6, *k3, p6; rep from * to end.

2nd row: K6, *p3, k6; rep from * to end.

Rep the last 2 rows twice more.

7th row: As 2nd row.

8th row: P6, *k3, p6; rep from * to end.

Rep the last 2 rows once more.

Rep these 10 rows.

'Faggotted' Rib

Multiple of 4 + 2.

1st row: K3, *yo, sl 1, k1, psso, k2; rep from * to last 3 sts, yo, sl 1, k1, psso, k1.

2nd row: P3, *yrn, p2tog, p2; rep from * to last 3 sts, yrn, p2tog, p1.

Rep these 2 rows.

Ripple Pattern

Multiple of 8 + 6.

1st row (right side): K6, *p2, k6; rep from * to end.

2nd row: K1, *p4, k4; rep from * to last 5 sts, p4, k1.

3rd row: P2, *k2, p2; rep from * to end.

4th row: P1, *k4, p4; rep from * to last 5 sts, k4, p1.

5th row: K2, *p2, k6; rep from * to last 4 sts, p2, k2.

6th row: P6, *k2, p6; rep from * to end.

7th row: As 4th row.

8th row: K2, *p2, k2; rep from * to end.

9th row: As 2nd row.

10th row: P2, *k2, p6; rep from * to last 4 sts, k2, p2.

Rep these 10 rows.

If you look at the same stripe series from the wrong side it looks completely different. Whereas on the right side there is a clear-cut color change, the wrong side has an interesting melange effect. If you know the cause and effect, this can be used deliberately as a lively element.

Mock Cable – Right

Multiple of 4 + 2.

1st row (right side): P2, *k2, p2; rep from * to end.

2nd row: K2, *p2, k2; rep from * to end.

3rd row: P2, *C2F, p2; rep from * to end.

4th row: As 2nd row.

Rep these 4 rows.

Cross Motif Pattern II

Worked as Cross Motif Pattern I on page 52, using
reverse side as right side.

Chevron Rib II

Multiple of 12 + 1.

1st row (right side): P2, k2, p2, k1, p2, k2, *p3, k2, p2, k1, p2, k2: rep from * to last 2 sts, p2.

2nd row: K2, p2, k2, p1, k2, p2, *k3, p2, k2, p1, k2, p2; rep from * to last 2 sts, k2.

3rd row: P1, *k2, p2, k3, p2, k2, p1; rep from * to end.

4th row: K1, *p2, k2, p3, k2, p2, k1; rep from * to end.

5th row: As 2nd row.

6th row: P2, k2, p2, k1, p2, k2, *p3, k2, p2, k1, p2, k2; rep from * to last 2 sts, p2.

7th row: As 4th row.

8th row: As 3rd row.

Rep these 8 rows.

Seed stitch gives a simple texture and a great firm fabric.

Diamond Eye

Multiple of 15.

1st row (right side): P1, k4, p5, k4, *p2, k4, p5, k4; rep from * to last st, p1.

2nd row: K2, p4, k3, p4, *k4, p4, k3, p4; rep from * to last 2 sts, k2.

3rd row: P3, k4, p1, k4, *p6, k4, p1, k4; rep from * to last 3 sts, p3.

4th row: K4, p7, *k8, p7; rep from * to last 4 sts, k4.

5th row: P5, k5, *p10, k5; rep from * to last 5 sts, p5.

6th row: P1, k5, p3, k5, *p2, k5, p3, k5; rep from * to last st, p1.

7th row: K2, p5, k1, p5, *k4, p5, k1, p5; rep from * to last 2 sts, k2.

8th row: P3, k9, *p6, k9; rep from * to last 3 sts, p3.

9th row: As 7th row.

10th row: As 6th row.

11th row: As 5th row.

12th row: As 4th row.

13th row: As 3rd row.

14th row: As 2nd row.

Rep these 14 rows.

Slipped Rib II

Multiple of 2 + 1.

1st row (right side): K1, *yo, sl 1 purlwise, yb, k1; rep
from * to end.

2nd row: Purl.

Rep these 2 rows.

Zigzag Moss Stitch

Multiple of 6 + 1.

1st row (right side): Knit.

2nd row: Purl.

3rd row: P1, *k5, p1; rep from * to end.

4th row: P1, *k1, p3, k1, p1; rep from * to end.

5th row: P1, *k1, p1; rep from * to end.

6th row: As 5th row.

7th row: K2, p1, k1, p1, *k3, p1, k1, p1; rep from * to last 2 sts, k2.

8th row: P3, k1, *p5, k1; rep from * to last 3 sts, p3.

9th row: Knit.

10th row: Purl.

11th row: K3, p1, *k5, p1; rep from * to last 3 sts, k3.

12th row: P2, k1, p1, k1, *p3, k1, p1, k1; rep from * to last 2 sts, p2.

13th row: K1, *p1, k1; rep from * to end.

14th row: As 13th row.

15th row: K1, *p1, k3, p1, k1; rep from * to end.

16th row: K1, *p5, k1; rep from * to end.

Rep these 16 rows.

Broken Diagonal Check

Multiple of 8.

1st row (right side): *K6, p2; rep from * to end.

2nd row: P1, *k2, p6; rep from * last 7 sts, k2, p5.

3rd row: K4, *p2, k6; rep from * to last 4 sts, p2, k2.

4th row: P3, *k2, p6; rep from * to last 5 sts, k2, p3.

5th row: K2, *p2, k6; rep from * to last 6 sts, p2, k4.

6th row: P5, *k2, p6; rep from * to last 3 sts, k2, p1.

7th row: Purl.

8th row: K2, *p6, k2; rep from * to last 6 sts, p6.

9th row: As 3rd row.

10th row: As 4th row.

11th row: As 5th row.

12th row: As 6th row.

13th row: *P2, k6; rep from * to end.

14th row: Knit.

Rep these 14 rows.

Reverse Fancy Diamond

Worked as Fancy Diamond pattern on page 209, using reverse as right side.

Pennant Stitch

Multiple of 5.

1st row (right side): Knit.

2nd row: *K1, p4; rep from * to end.

3rd row: *K3, p2; rep from * to end.

4th row: As 3rd row.

5th row: As 2nd row.

Knit 2 rows.

8th row: *P4, k1; rep from * to end.

9th row: *P2, k3; rep from * to end.

10th row: As 9th row.

11th row: As 8th row.

12th row: Knit.

Rep these 12 rows.

Fancy Slip Stitch Rib

Multiple of 5 + 2.

1st row (right side): P2, *k1, sl 1 purlwise, k1, p2; rep from * to end.

2nd row: K2, *p3, k2; rep from * to end.

Rep these 2 rows.

Parallelogram Check

Multiple of 10.

1st row (right side): *K5, p5; rep from * to end.

2nd row: K4, *p5, k5; rep from * to last 6 sts, p5, k1.

3rd row: P2, *k5, p5; rep from * to last 8 sts, k5, p3.

4th row: K2, *p5, k5; rep from * to last 8 sts, p5, k3.

5th row: P4, *k5, p5; rep from * to last 6 sts, k5, p1.

6th row: *P5, k5; rep from * to end.

Rep these 6 rows.

Contrary Fisherman's Rib

Multiple of 2 + 1.

Foundation row: Knit.

1st row (right side): Sl 1, *K1B, k1; rep from * to end.

2nd row: Sl 1, *k1, K1B; rep from * to last 2 sts, k2.

3rd row: As 1st row.

4th row: As 2nd row.

5th row: As 1st row.

6th row: Sl 1, *K1B, k1; rep from * to end.

7th row: As 2nd row.

8th row: As 6th row.

9th row: As 2nd row.

10th row: As 6th row.

Rep the last 10 rows only.

Herringbone Texture

Multiple of 16 + 1.

1st row (right side): [K2, p2] twice, k1, p2, k2, p2, *k3, p2, k2, p2, k1, p2, k2, p2; rep from * to last 2 sts, k2.

2nd row: P1, *k2, p2, k2, p3, k2, p2, k2, p1; rep from * to end.

3rd row: K1, *p1, k2, p2, k5, p2, k2, p1, k1; rep from * to end.

4th row: P3, k2, p2, k1, p1, k1, p2, k2, *p5, k2, p2, k1, p1, k1, p2, k2; rep from * to last 3 sts, p3.

Rep these 4 rows.

Double Mock Ribbing

Multiple of 4 + 2.

1st row (wrong side): K2, *p2, k2; rep from * to end.

2nd row: P2, *keeping yarn at front of work sl 2 purlwise, p2; rep from * to end.

Rep these 2 rows.

Diagonal Seed Stitch

Multiple of 6.

1st row (right side): *K5, p1; rep from * to end.

2nd row: P1, *k1, p5; rep from * to last 5 sts, k1, p4.

3rd row: K3, *p1, k5; rep from * to last 3 sts, p1, k2.

4th row: P3, *k1, p5; rep from * to last 3 sts, k1, p2.

5th row: K1, *p1, k5; rep from * to last 5 sts, p1, k4.

6th row: *P5, k1; rep from * to end.

Rep these 6 rows.

Mock Wavy Cable Rib

Multiple of 4 + 2.

1st row (right side): P2, *k2, p2; rep from * to end.

2nd and every alt row: K2, *p2, k2; rep from * to end.

3rd row: P2, *C2B, p2; rep from * to end.

5th row: As 1st row.

7th row: P2, *k2tog but do not slip off needle, then insert right-hand needle between these 2 sts and knit the 1st st again, slipping both sts off needle tog, p2; rep from * to end.

8th row: As 2nd row.

Rep these 8 rows.

Raindrop

Multiple of 6 + 3.

Note: Slip sts purlwise with yarn at back of work (wrong side) = S on diagram.

Foundation row: K1, p1, *k2, p1; rep from * to last st, k1.

1st row (right side): K1, sl 1, *k2, sl 1; rep from * to last st, k1.

2nd row: K1, p1, *k2, p1; rep from * to last st, k1.

Rep the last 2 rows once more.

5th row: K1, sl 1, *k5, sl 1; rep from * to last st, k1.

6th row: K1, p1, *k5, p1; rep from * to last st, k1.

Rep the last 2 rows once more.

9th and 10th rows: As 1st and 2nd rows.

Rep the last 2 rows once more.

13th row: K4, sl 1, *k5, sl 1; rep from * to last 4 sts, k4.

14th row: K4, p1, *k5, p1; rep from * to last 4 sts, k4.

Rep the last 2 rows once more.

Rep the last 16 rows.

Piqué Triangles

Multiple of 5.

1st row (right side): *P1, k4; rep from * to end.

2nd row: *P3, k2; rep from * to end.

3rd row: As 2nd row.

4th row: *P1, k4; rep from * to end.

Rep these 4 rows.

Once you have selected your stitch do a gauge swatch before starting your project.

Diamond Leaves

Multiple of 15 + 2.

1st row (right side): P6, k2, p1, k2, *p10, k2, p1, k2; rep from * to last 6 sts, p6.

2nd row: K6, p2, k1, p2, *k10, p2, k1, p2; rep from * to last 6 sts, k6.

Rep the last 2 rows once more.

5th row: P5, k2, p3, k2, *p8, k2, p3, k2; rep from * to last 5 sts, p5.

6th row: K5, p2, k3, p2, *k8, p2, k3, p2; rep from * to last 5 sts, k5.

Rep the last 2 rows once more.

9th row: P4, k2, p2, k1, p2, k2, *p6, k2, p2, k1, p2, k2; rep from * to last 4 sts, p4.

10th row: K4, p2, k2, p1, k2, p2, *k6, p2, k2, p1, k2, p2; rep from * to last 4 sts, k4.

Rep the last 2 rows once more.

13th row: P3, k2, p2, k1, p1, k1, p2, k2, *p4, k2, p2, k1, p1, k1, p2, k2; rep from * to last 3 sts, p3.

14th row: K3, p2, k2, p1, k1, p1, k2, p2, *k4, p2, k2, p1, k1, p1, k2, p2; rep from * to last 3 sts, k3.

Rep the last 2 rows once more.

17th row: P2, *k2, p2, k1, [p1, k1] twice, p2, k2, p2; rep from * to end.

18th row: K2, *p2, k2, p1, [k1, p1] twice, k2, p2, k2; rep from * to end.

Rep the last 2 rows once more.

21st and 22nd rows: As 13th and 14th rows.

Rep these 2 rows once more.

25th and 26th rows: As 9th and 10th rows.

Rep these 2 rows once more.

29th and 30th rows: As 5th and 6th rows.

Rep these 2 rows once more.

Rep these 32 rows.

Mosaic Stitch

Multiple of 10 + 7.

1st row (right side): P3, *k1, p3, k1, p1, k1, p3; rep from * to last 4 sts, k1, p3.

2nd row: K3, *p1, k3, p1, k1, p1, k3; rep from * to last 4 sts, p1, k3.

Rep the last 2 rows once more.

5th row: P2, *k1, p1, k1, p3, k1, p3; rep from * to last 5 sts, k1, p1, k1, p2.

6th row: K2, *p1, k1, p1, k3, p1, k3; rep from * to last 5 sts, p1, k1, p1, k2.

Rep the last 2 rows once more.

Rep these 8 rows.

resources

Rowan

Westminster Fibers, Inc

3, Northern Boulevard

Suite 3

Amherst

NH 03031

www.westminsterfibers.com

Other titles currently available in the Harmony Guides series:

index

abbreviations

[ ]	work instructions within brackets as many times as directed
( )	work instructions within parentheses in the place directed
*	repeat instructions following the single asterisk as directed
* *	repeat instructions following the asterisks as directed
alt	alternate
C2B	cable 2 back
C2F	cable 2 front
C2L	cross 2 left
C3L	cross 3 left
C2P	cross 2 purl
C2R	cross 2 right
C3R	cross 3 right
C3	cross 3
cm	centimeter(s)
in	inch(es)
k	knit
K1B	knit 1 below
K1B Back	from the top, insert point of right-hand needle into back of stitch below next stitch on left-hand needle and knit it
k2tog	knit 2 together
KB1	knit into back of next stitch
MB	make bobble
p	purl
p2tog	purl 2 together
PB1	purl into back of next stitch
psso	pass slip stitch over
rep	repeat(s)
RS	right side
sl	slip
St st	stockinette stitch
st(s)	stitch(es)
T2B	twist 2 back
T2F	twist 2 front
tbl	through back loop
tog	together
WS	wrong side
yb	yarn to the back
yf	yarn to the front
yfon	yarn forward and over needle (increase)
yfrn	with yarn in front (increase)
yon	yarn over needle (increase)
yrn	yarn around needle (increase)